ASSYRIAN PRIMER
AND ASSYRIAN TEXTS

Groom with horses. Relief from Kouyunjik.

ASSYRIAN PRIMER AND ASSYRIAN TEXTS

INDUCTIVE METHOD OF LEARNING THE CUNEIFORM CHARACTERS AND READING THE INSCRIPTIONS

By

J. DYNELEY PRINCE, Ph.D.

And

ERNEST A. BUDGE, M.R.A.S.

ARES PUBLISHERS INC.

CHICAGO MCMLXXVIII

Figure of the king. Nimroud.

This is the First Edition
Combining in One Volume

The *Assyrian Primer*
in an unchanged reprint of the edition:
New York, 1909
The *Assyrian Texts*
is an exact reprint of the edition:
London, 1880
ARES PUBLISHERS INC.
612 N. Michigan Avenue
Chicago, Illinois 60611
Printed in the United States of America
International Standard Book Number:
0-89005-226-3

ASSYRIAN PRIMER

AN

INDUCTIVE METHOD

OF LEARNING THE CUNEIFORM CHARACTERS

BY

J. DYNELEY PRINCE, PH.D.

PROFESSOR OF SEMITIC LANGUAGES IN COLUMBIA UNIVERSITY

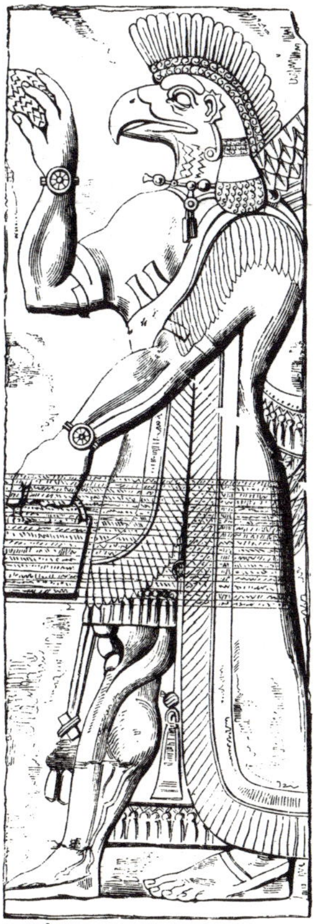

Winged eagle-headed figure. Nimroud

. Sacred tree with standing figures. Kouyunjik.

Sacred tree with kneeling figures. Kouyunjik.

Foreword

The need of a series of progressive lessons for beginners in Cuneiform has long been felt in the Columbia University Semitic Department. The object of the present work is to lighten the labours of the English speaking Assyrian student, who has hitherto been compelled to learn, by sheer force of memory, the ninety-eight simple signs before he could proceed to read the most ordinary text. In the following lessons an attempt has been made to grade the acquisition of the signs and the learning of the main features of the grammar, so that the student may proceed, inductively and with comparative facility, to master simultaneously both the intricacies of the characters and the most salient facts of Assyrian grammatical structure.

My especial thanks are due to my friend Dr. Robert J. Lau of Columbia University for the great care and skill with which he has autographed the sign-lists and exercises.

J. Dyneley Prince.

Columbia University, New York.

Relief from Nimroud.

Part I.

The Assyro-Babylonian system of writing is not alphabetic, but syllabic and ideographic. This work is devoted mainly to the exposition of the purely syllabic signs which are divisible into two categories: viz., simple syllables, or those which contain only one consonant, as ba, ab, treated in Part I., and compound syllables, or those which contain two consonants as bab, giš, treated in Part II. The following Signlist I. of 97 signs, arranged for mnemonic purposes according to similarity in form, gives all the simple syllables, which must be thoroughly learned in the first nine graded lessons before proceeding to the study of the compound and ideographic characters in Part II.

The student should observe the following system of transliteration based on the Hebrew alphabet:

$\aleph_1$ = א = ʾ; $\aleph_2$ = ה = ʾ; $\aleph_3$ = ח = ḫ; $\aleph_4$ = ע = ʿ; $\aleph_5$ = ע̇ = gh; ב = b; ג = g; ד = d; ז = z; ט = ṭ; כ = k; ל = l; מ = m; נ = n; ס = s; פ = p; ק = q; ר = r; שׁ = š; ת = t.

Rules for reading

I. A strict rule was followed in syllabic writing which was rarely departed from: viz., in cases where one of the syllabic signs has a varied consonantal value (as *ad*, *aṭ*, *at*) and is followed by a sign with a fixed consonantal value, the fixed consonantal value prevails for both signs. Thus in 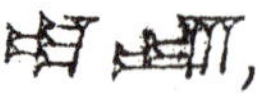, the sign  may be read alone as *ad*, *aṭ*, or *at*, but, as it is followed here by the fixed consonantal value *ta*, the word must be read *at-ta* and not *ad-ta*, nor *aṭ-ta*.

Again, the word *ug-ga-tu* =  must be read thus, and not *uk-ga-tu*, nor *uḳ-ga-tu*, because the fixed value *ga* follows  = *ug*, *uk*, *uḳ*.

II. Furthermore, a syllable ending in a vowel at the beginning of a word is apt to be followed by a syllable beginning with the same or a kindred vowel: e.g., *ga-aš-ru*, but *ri-e-šu* must be read *rêšu*, since the vowel-combination *i-e* was used to denote long *ê*.

III. When in the sign-list a value is enclosed in parentheses, as 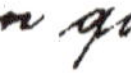 = *bu* (*pu*), this indicates that the value in question is not to be chosen, unless especially demanded by an adjacent fixed consonantal value, or by the word-root given in the glossary.

IV. It will be observed that several signs are identical in value, in which case the transliteration differentiates between them by arbitrarily affixing accents. Thus,  = <u>šu</u>, but = <u>šú</u>; 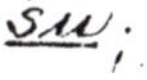 = <u>u</u>;  = <u>ú</u>;  = <u>ù</u>. This does not imply a difference in pronunciation.

V. Every new sign in the graded lessons is numbered in accordance with the enumeration in the tables, in order to facilitate a speedy identification. The reverse table in Part I. must be used in translating the exercises from English into cuneiform. The grammatical references are all to the English edition of Delitzsch's Assyrian Grammar = D. Gr.

VI. The student should constantly refer to the glossary at the close of this work, where all the Assyrian words used in the primer are arranged in Roman transliteration in the order of the Hebrew alphabet. For example, in determining the values of such a word as , which may be read <u>da-a-</u>

bu or ta-a-bu, a reference to the glossary under דוב will show that there is no word da-a-bu in this list. The next alternative is of course to refer to טוב = ta-a-bu 'good'. Again,  may be read ab-lu or ap-lu, but the latter word alone is indicated in the glossary, so also with 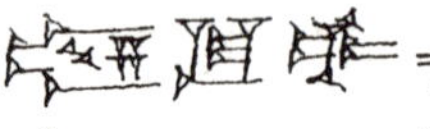 = as-ku-up from סכף and not from סכב, etc. In fact, this principle of choice by exclusion is the chief feature of this decipherment, until the student has become sufficiently familiar with the Assyrian vocabulary to tell the value of a doubtful word at a glance, by his knowledge of the root.

Sign-List I.

Signs with simple values.

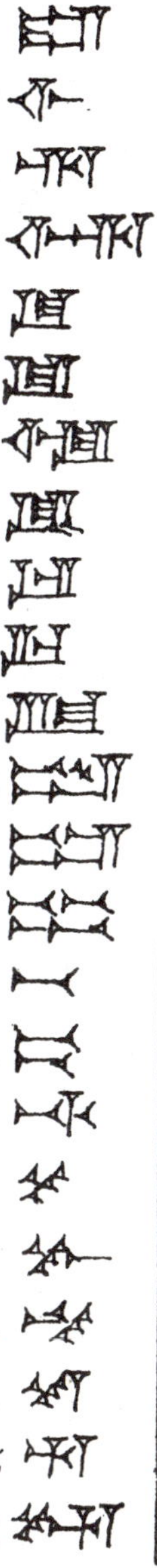

No.	Value	No.	Value
1.	a	24.	ra
2.	e	25.	ši
3.	ba	26.	ri
4.	gu	27.	ar
5.	su	28.	ku
6.	zi	29.	lu
7.	gi	30.	ù
8.	ni	31.	qi
9.	ir	32.	ib, (ip)
10.	sa	33.	ur
11.	ez, iz, iṣ	34.	ṭu
12.	pa	35.	il
13.	ma	36.	úr
14.	aš	37.	qu
15.	la	38.	be
16.	ad, aṭ, at	39.	bi
17.	ṣi	40.	ti
18.	i	41.	še
19.	ịa	42.	bu (pu)
20.	du	43.	mu
21.	uš	44.	te
22.	iš	45.	hu
23.	si	46.	uz, uṣ

No.	Sign	Value	No.	Sign	Value
47.		ig, ik, (iq)	73.		pi
48.		ḫi (ṭi)	74.		na
49.		= 𒄭	75.		áš, (rú)
50.		aḫ, iḫ, uḫ	76.		an
51.		im	77.		qa
52.		am	78.		me
53.		ṭe, ne	79.		nu
54.		ša	80.		šú
55.		di, (ṭi)	81.		en
56.		ki (qi)	82.		u
57.		az, as, aṣ	83.		ga
58.		ug, uk (uq)	84.		ta
59.		šu	85.		in
60.		da, (ṭa)	86.		se
61.		id, iṭ, it	87.		gu
62.		za, ṣa	88.		ub (up), ár
63.		ḫa	89.		el
64.		un	90.		ṣu
65.		ú	91.		ab, (ap)
66.		eš	92.		um
67.		mi	93.		ag, ak, (aq)
68.		pú	94.		ka
69.		ša	95.		ul
70.		li	96.		al
71.		tu	97.		ru
72.		ud, uṭ, ut, tu	98.		ád.

Reverse Table of Simple Values.

ℵ —	49
a	1
ab	91
ag	93
ad	16
ád	98
az	57
aḫ	50
aṭ	16
ak̇	93
al	96
am	52
an	76
as	57
(ap)	91
aṣ	57
(aq)	93
ar	27
(ár)	88
aš	14
áš	75
at	16
e	2
ez	11
el	89
en	81
eš	56
ba	3
be	38
bi	39
bu	42
ga	83
gi	7
gu	87
da	60
di	55
du	20
u	82
ú	65
ù	30
ub	88
ug	58
ud	72
uz	46
uḫ	50
uṭ	72
uk̇	58
ul	95
um	92
un	54
(up)	88
uṣ	46
(uq)	58
ur	33
úr	36
uš	21
ut	72
za	62
zi	6
zu	4
ḫa	63
ḫi	48
ḫu	43
ṭa	60
ṭe	53
ṭi	55, 48
ṭu	34
i	18
i̯a	19
ib	32
ig	47
id	61
iz	11
iḫ	50
iṭ	61
ik̇	47
il	35
im	51
in	85
ip	32
iṣ	11
(iq)	47
ir	9
iš	22
it	61
ka	94
ki	56
ku	28
la	15
li	70
lu	29
ma	13
me	78
mi	67
mu	43
na	74
ne	53
ni	8
nu	79
sa	10
se	86
si	23
su	5
pa	12
pi	73
(pu)	42
pú	68
ṣa	62
ṣi	17
ṣu	90
qa	77
qi	31 (56)
qu	37
ra	24
ri	26
ru	97
(rú)	75
ša	54
šá	69
še	41
ši	25
šu	59
šú	80
ta	84
te	44
ti	40
tu	71, 72

Lesson I.

Note that there is no article, definite nor indefinite.

The Personal Pronoun.

Signs	Meaning
1 74 28	'I'
16 84	'thou'
16 40	'thou' (fem.)
59 82	'he'
59 65	" (alternate forms)
80 65	" (alternate forms)
25 18	'she'
1 8 79	'we'
1 8 8	" (alternate forms)
8 2 79	" (alternate forms)
8 18 8	" (alternate forms)
8 8	" (alternate forms)
16 71 79	'you'
59 79	'they (masc.)'
59 82 79	" (alternate forms)
80 82 79	" (alternate forms)
25 74	'they' (fem.)

Signs	Meaning
1 42	'father'
1 42 40	'fathers' (irreg. plur.)

Write a transliteration of the above

words learning at the same time the signs, the numbers above which refer to the sign-table (D. Gr. § 55a).

Transliterate and translate the following exercise into Assyrian, noting that the copula is not expressed in Assyrian:

I (am a) father. Thou (art a) father. He (is a) father. We (are) fathers. They (masc.) (are) fathers.

Lesson II.

Possession and Prepositions.

Note that the tone falls always on a long syllable as a-a, u-u (in a-bu-u-ti 'fathers', pron. abûti), or on a doubled syllable, as ad-di, pron. áddi.

Possession is expressed by suffixes as follows:

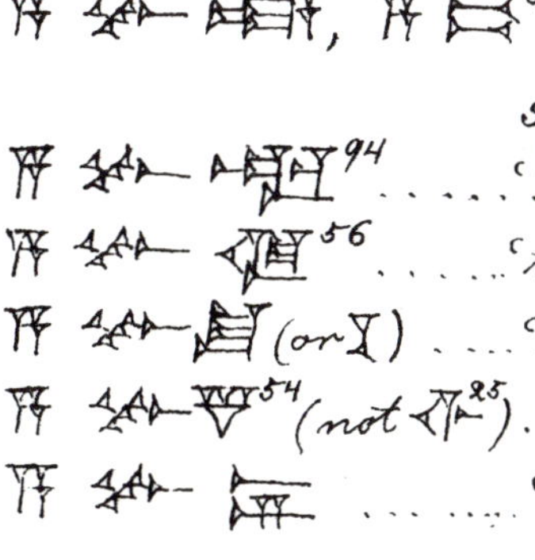

'my father (The 1p. sfx. is -i or -ia).

.... 'thy father'.

..... 'thy (fem.) father'.

.... 'his father'.

'her father.'

.... 'our father'.

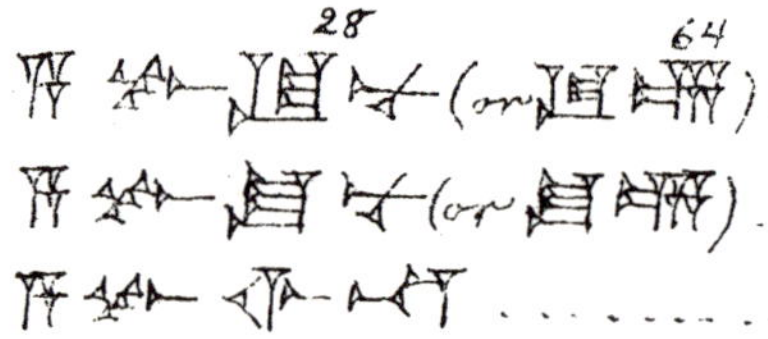

...'your father'.
...'their father'.
...'their (fem.) father'.
D. Gr. §56.

There are three cases: nominative ending in *-u*, genitive ending in *-i* (or *e*), and accusative ending in *-a*, which, when not followed by a suffix, may also have a final *-m*; e. g. *um*, *im*, *am* (see Lesson VIII). This phenomenon, which has no perceptible meaning, is called "mimation". For ex., *a-bu* (or *a-bu-um*), gen. *a-bi* (or *a-bi-im*, acc. *a-ba* (or *a-ba-am*). D. Gr. § 66. It should be observed at this point that especially in the later literature the rules for case were very loosely followed.

Prepositions invariably govern the genitive case, as *a-na a-bi* 'unto the father'. This is also true when the possessive suffix follows the noun as *a-na a-bi-ia* 'to my father'; *a-na a-bi-šu* 'to his father', etc. The pronominal suffixes are used with all the following prepositions, save *a-na*, *i-na*, *iš-tu*, *ul-tu*, and *ki-ma*. Thus, we may say *it-ti-ia* 'with me', *it-ti-ka* 'with thee', but not <u>a-na-ia</u>, <u>a-na-ka</u>.

Prepositions.

-  ... 'unto, to'.
- 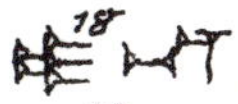 ... 'in'.
- 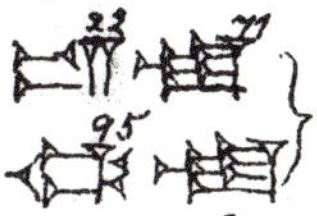 ... 'from, out of'.
- 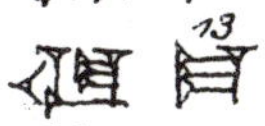 ... 'like'.
-  ... 'with'.
-  ... 'upon'.
-  ... 'with me'.
-  ... 'with thee', etc.
-  ... 'upon me', etc. D. Gr. § 81a.
-  ... 'of'.

Lesson III.

Vocabulary.

- 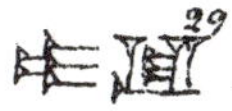 ... 'god'.
-  ... 'gods'.
-  ... 'one'.
- 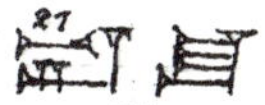 ... 'foundation'.
-  ... 'man = <u>homo</u>'.
-  ... 'men'.
-  ... 'man = <u>vir</u>'.
- 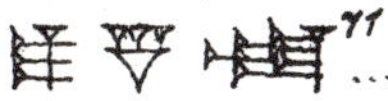 ... 'woman, wife' (see Lesson VIII)
- 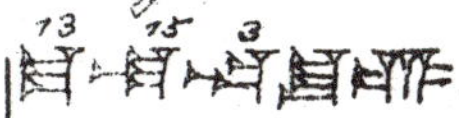 ... 'as many as there are'.
-  ... 'eye'.
- , or 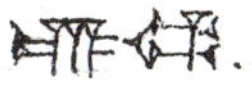 ... 'not'.
-  ... 'not'.
- 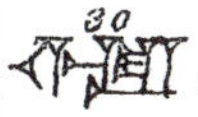 or  ... 'and'.
- 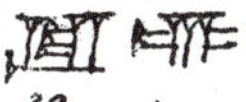 ... 'verily'.
-  ... 'house'.
-  ... 'earth'.

Reading Exercise.

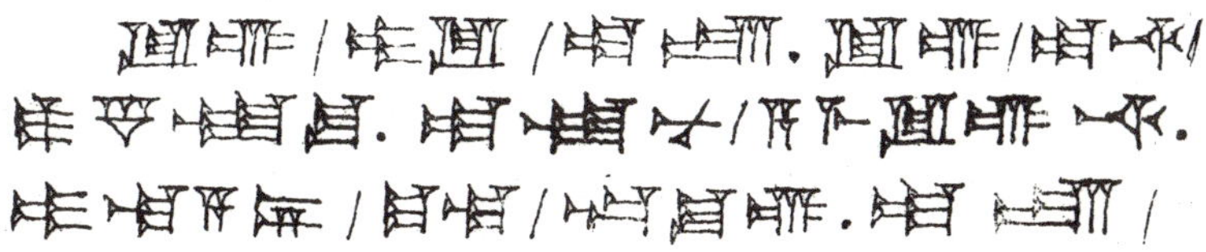

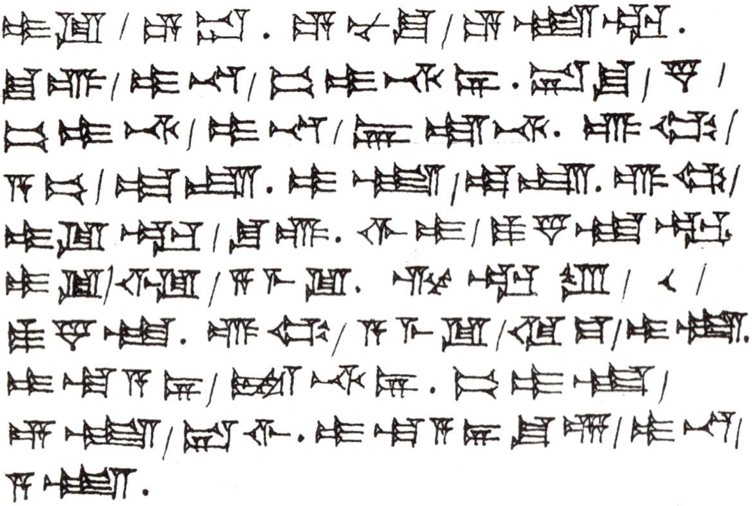

Observe that the particles ul and lu-u usually precede the nouns which they govern; as ul a-me-lu at-ta not a man (art) thou; lu-u aš-ša-tu at-ti verily a woman (art) thou (fem.).

Translate into Assyrian.

Your god (is) one. Verily, they (are) gods. The house of the man. Her eye (is) upon us. The foundation of thy (fem.) house is in the earth. The wife of the man (is) not with me. Verily, the gods (are) not men. Verily, the eye of the god (is) upon the earth. The men, as many as there are. Their wives (are) with your men.

Lesson IV.

Separable Pronominal Forms, Adjectives and Plurals.

As stated in Lesson II., the prepositions a-na, i-na, iš-tu, ul-tu, and ki-ma cannot take the pronominal suffixes. These prepositions are construed with the following separable pronominal oblique forms:

	'me'.	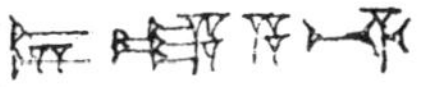	'us'.
	'thee'.		'you'.
	'thee' (fem.)		'them' (masc.).
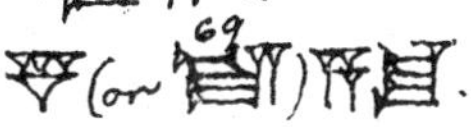	'him'.		The fem. 3 p. pl. separable pronoun has not been found. D. Gr. § 55 b.
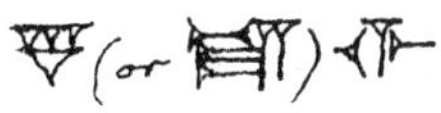	'her'.		

Masculine nouns take their plurals usually in -e (or -i) for all cases; as uš-šu 'foundation', pl. uš-še or uš-ši-e (=še), but a number of such nouns make the plural in -a-ni; notably a-lu 'city', i-lu 'god', ša-ar-ru 'king', ma-al-ku 'prince' and du-u-ru 'wall'. A few other masculine nouns use the adjectival plural ending -u-ti (te); as a-bu 'father', pl. a-bu-u-ti (also a-bi-e = a-bê); a-me-lu 'man', pl. a-me-lu-u-ti (see Lesson II.); D. Gr. § 44.

Feminine nouns are known in the singular commonly, although not always, by the suffix

-tu, as *ma-al-ku* 'prince', but *ma-al-ka-tu* 'princess'. This *-tu* however is joined to the noun by means of the auxiliary vowel *-a-* when two consonants would come together, as *malkatu*. An exception is the noun *li-ša-nu* 'tongue', pl. *li-ša-na-a-ti* and a number of other substantives; D. Gr. § 68. Feminine nouns make their plural invariably for all cases by the endings *-a-ti* (*-tɛ*)[44-45] and *ɛ-ti* (*-tɛ*). Thus *ma-al-ka-a-ti* 'princesses'; *a-ḫa-a-tu* 'sister', pl. *a-ḫa-a-ti* (*tɛ*), and *ɛ-mɛ-tu* 'mother in law', pl. *ɛ-mɛ-ɛ-ti* (*tɛ*); D. Gr. § 69. It is sometimes difficult for the learner to distinguish between the genitive singular of a fem. noun and the plural, but this may always be determined by the context.

Adjectives do not differ in form from nouns except in their masc. plural. They usually follow and must agree with the nouns qualified in gender, number and case. The fem. sing. adjective like the average fem. noun ends in *-tu*, (*a-tu*), as *ṭa-a-bu* 'good'; fem. *ṭa-ab-tu*. Thus *ma-al-ku ṭa-a-bu* 'a good prince', but *ma-al-ka-tu ṭa-ab-tu* 'a good princess'; gen. *ma-al-ki ṭa-a-bi*; fem. *ma-al-ka-ti ṭa-ab-ti*, etc.

Masculine adjectives usually take their

plural in -u-ti (tē[44]). Thus, ma-al-ka-a-ni ṭa-bu-u-ti 'good princes'; uš-še ṭa-bu-u-ti 'good foundations'. Feminine adjectives invariably make their plural in -a-ti (tē) or e-ti (tē); thus ma-al-ka-a-ti ṭa-ba-a-ti (tē) 'good princesses.'

Vocabulary.

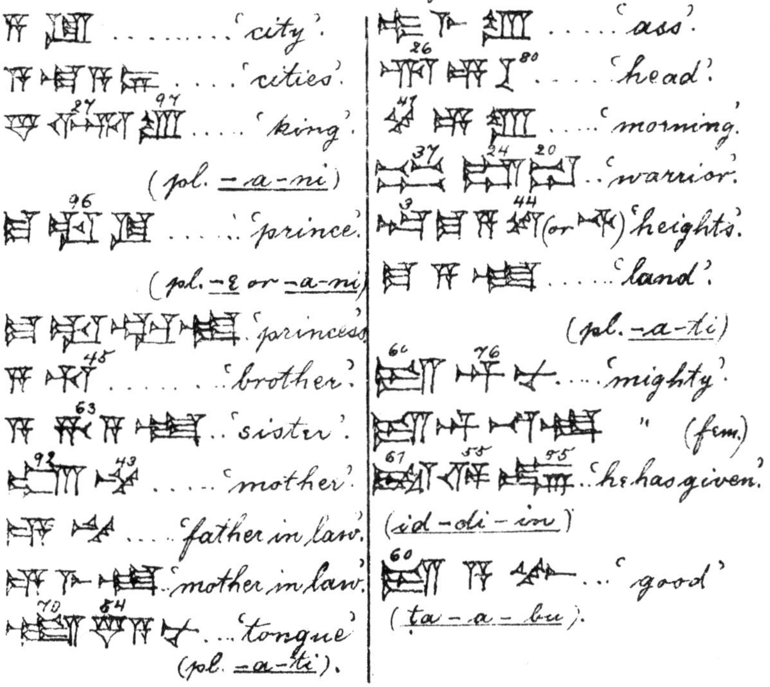
'city'.
'cities'.
'king'.
(pl. -a-ni)
'prince'.
(pl. -ē or -a-ni)
'princess'
'brother'.
'sister'.
'mother'.
'father in law'.
'mother in law'.
'tongue'
(pl. -a-ti).
'ass'.
'head'.
'morning'.
'warrior'.
(or) 'heights'.
'land'.
(pl. -a-ti)
'mighty'.
" (fem.)
'he has given'.
(id-di-in)
'good'
(ṭa-a-bu).

Lesson V.

Reading Exercise.

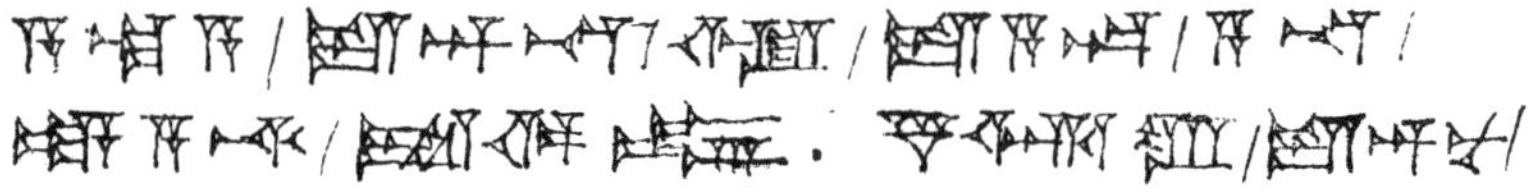

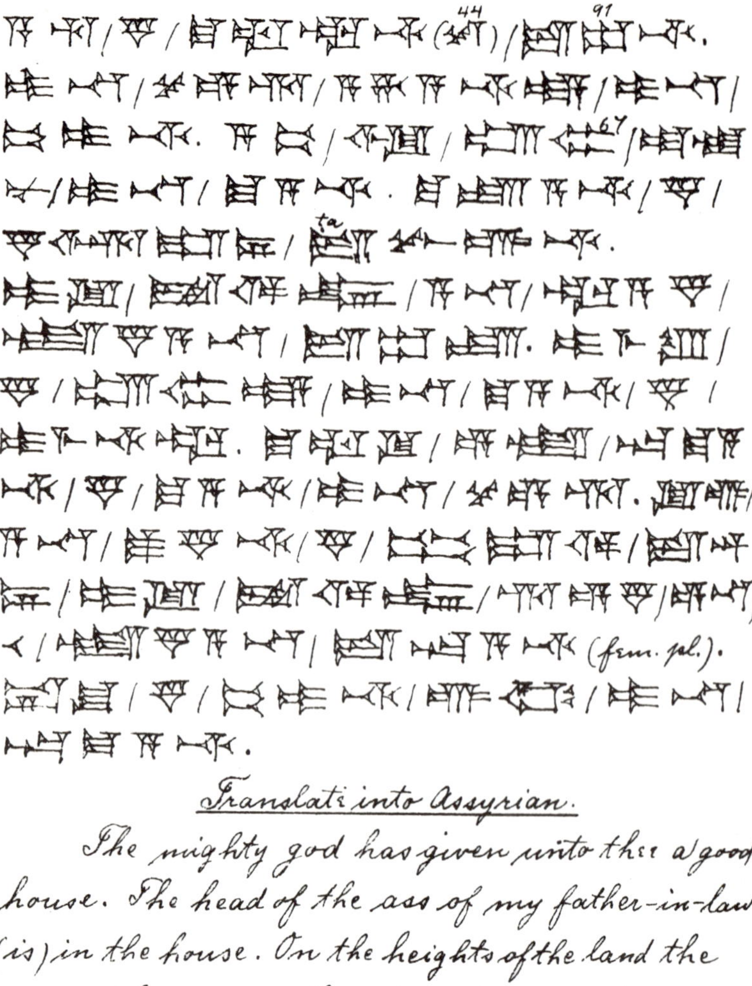

Translate into Assyrian.

The mighty god has given unto thee a good house. The head of the ass of my father-in-law (is) in the house. On the heights of the land the prince has given the city unto us (unto you, unto them). My mother, thou (art) a good woman! Kings and princes, warriors and cities he has given unto thee (fem.). In the morning my head is good. Princesses and women, men and warriors. The brother of her father gave the ass to the princess. I (am) thy king and thy prince. She (is) his wife and his princess. The good sister (is) with the king and the warrior. The good sisters (are) with the kings and the warriors.

Lesson VI.

Genitive Apposition. Demonstr. Pronouns.

The genitive relation in Assyrian may be expressed in two ways: viz., either by the preposition ša 'of', followed by the genitive case, as bi-i-tu ša a-me-li 'the house of the man;' or by the juxtaposition of two nouns, the first of which takes the construct state as in Hebrew; cf. bi-it a-me-li 'the house of the man.'

The construct (D.G. §72) is formed primarily by the omission of the case ending. Thus a-me-lu 'man'; constr. a-me-el; bi-i-tu 'house', constr. bi-it. When a noun ends in the feminine -tu, as ma-al-ka-tu 'princess', the constr. is ma-al-ka-at[16], the characteristic fem. -t- being retained. In the case of the segholate nouns, the construct is formed by the omission of the case-ending and insertion between the second and third consonants of the characteristic vowel of the segholate; thus *ṣa-al-mu* 'image', constr. *ṣa-la-am*; *ši-ip-ru* 'message', constr. *ši-pi[73]-ir*; *uz[46]-nu* 'ear', constr. *u-zŭ[4]-un*. Nouns of the class of *ma-al-ku* 'prince' (really = *ma-li-ku*) make the construct as in *ma-li-ik*.[47]

The construct plural may be formed by dropping the *i* ending of masc. *a-ni*, *u-ti* and fem. *a-ti*, although this principle is not always observed. Thus *ša-ar-ra-ni ma-a-ti* (generally) 'kings of the land' or *ša-ar-ra-an* (seldom); *ma-ta-a-ti ša-ar-ri* 'the lands of the king', but very often *ma-ta-at ša-ar-ri*. The adj. masc. pl. *-u-ti* also frequently becomes *ut* in the construct. The ordinary masc. plural ending in *-e* (*-i*) does not alter for the construct at all. Thus *ma-al-ki* (*e*) *ma-ta-a-ti* 'princes of the land.'

The Demonstrative Pronouns (D. Gr. § 57) given in the next vocabulary must follow the nouns which they qualify. Thus: *ša-ar-ru šu-a-tu* 'that king'; *ma-al-ka-tu ši-a-ti* 'that princess'. Context alone will aid the learner to distinguish between the relative pronoun *ša* (D. Gr. § 58) and the prep. *ša* 'of'.

Note that relative possession is expressed as in Hebrew: ša-ar-ru ša bi-tu-šu ṭa-a-bu 'the king whose (who-his) house is good' (bi-i-tu is a masculine in the sing. but has fem. pl. bi-ta-a-ti).

Lesson VII.

Vocabulary.

[cuneiform] .... 'image' (ṣa-al-mu); constr. [cuneiform]
[cuneiform] .... 'message' (ši-ip-ru); constr. [cuneiform]
[cuneiform] .... 'road'; constr. [cuneiform]
[cuneiform] .... 'greeting, peace'; constr. [cuneiform]
[cuneiform] .... 'I conquered' (ak-šu-ud).
[cuneiform] .... 'marsh.'
[cuneiform] (ik) 'he went.'
[cuneiform] (id) [cuneiform] .... 'he looked.'
[cuneiform] (aṣ) [cuneiform] (up) 'I overthrew'.
[cuneiform] .... 'entirety'; used in constr. for 'all'.
[cuneiform] .... 'eighth'.
[cuneiform] .... 'I stand'.
[cuneiform] ...... 'way, road'.
[cuneiform] ...... 'hand.'

[cuneiform] (tu); [cuneiform] (masc.) 'that.' [cuneiform] (fem.)
[cuneiform] (masc.), [cuneiform] (fem.) 'those'.
[cuneiform] (masc.), [cuneiform] (fem.) 'this.'

〔cuneiform〕 (or 〔cuneiform〕) .... 'these' (masc.).

〔cuneiform〕 (or 〔cuneiform〕) .... " (fem.).

〔cuneiform〕 ...rel. pron. 'who, which, what' (all genders and numbers).

〔cuneiform〕 .... 'who?' (inten.).

〔cuneiform〕[67] .... 'what?' (inten.).

Exercise.

〔cuneiform text〕

〔cuneiform text〕

〔cuneiform text〕

〔cuneiform text〕

〔cuneiform text〕[48]

〔cuneiform text〕

〔cuneiform text〕

〔cuneiform text〕(=at)[16] 〔cuneiform〕[89]

〔cuneiform text〕

〔cuneiform text〕

〔cuneiform text〕

〔cuneiform text〕

〔cuneiform text〕

〔cuneiform text〕[17]

〔cuneiform text〕 〔cuneiform〕[4] 〔cuneiform〕[64]

〔cuneiform text〕

〔cuneiform text〕

〔cuneiform text〕

〔cuneiform text〕

〔cuneiform text〕

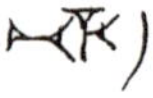

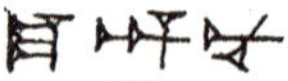

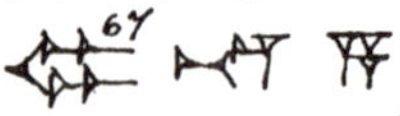

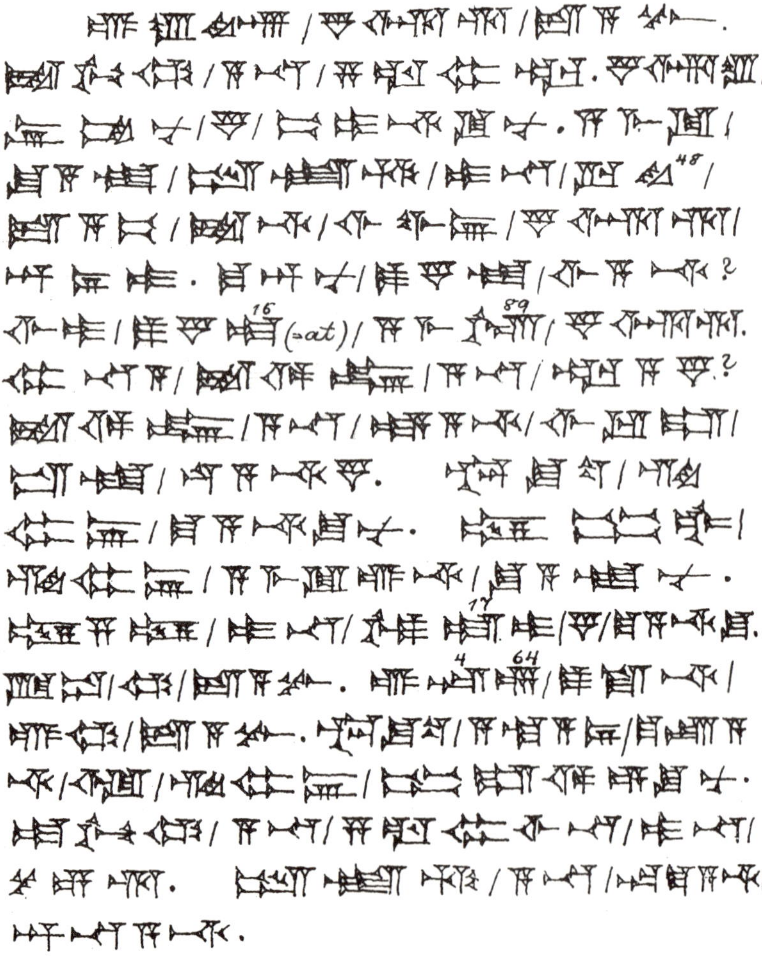

Translate into Assyrian.

The good king went unto the house of those men, and he looked at (a-na) the image of the warrior of the city. The roads of this city (are) not good. They (are a) marsh. What did the king give unto us? He gave to me his hand. My greeting unto you. I overthrew all the warriors of this city. Who (are) they? They (are) the princes and princesses whose images I looked at (lit. who I looked at their images). The greeting of all the kings (is) good. I stand in the eighth house. I have conquered these cities and those warriors. He gave unto me the message of the woman who (is) in that house. Your father (is) a king and a prince. My greeting unto him.

Lesson VIII.

Abstracts, Mimation & Adverbs.

Abstracts are formed most commonly from nouns by the fem. ending -u-tu constr. -ut, as ša-ar-ru 'king'; ša-ar-ru-u-tu 'kingdom, royalty'; pa-at-ru 'dagger'; pa-aṭ-ru-u-tu 'right to carry a dagger'; ap-lu 'son'; ap-lu-u-tu 'sonship', etc. When the possessive suffixes are attached to this ending, the case-vowel is usually dropped and the *š* of the suffix becomes *s*. Thus for *ša-ar-ru-tu-šu* 'his kingdom' we may write *ša-ar-ru-ut-su*^{5}, etc.

In Lesson II. the phenomenon of mimation was mentioned according to which the case-vowel may take an additional *m*; as nom. *ša-ar-ru-um*, gen. *ša-ar-ri-im*; acc. *ša-ar-ra-am*. When, however, to a vowel thus mimated, the possessive suffix is added, the mimation disappears; as *ša-ar-ru-um* but *ša-ar-ru-šu* 'his king', rarely in Assyrian *ša-ar-ru-um-šu*. This mimation has no signification like Arabic *Tanwin* which gives an indefinite character to the noun.

Adverbs are often formed from adjectives by the suffix *-iš*, as *ṭa-a-bi-iš* 'well' from *ṭa-a-bu* 'good'; *ra-bi-iš* 'greatly' from *ra-bu-u* 'great', etc; D. Gr. § 80 b. Adverbial expressions are also formed by means of prepositions and nouns, as *a-na da-ra-a-ti* or *da-ri-iš*.

Vocabulary.

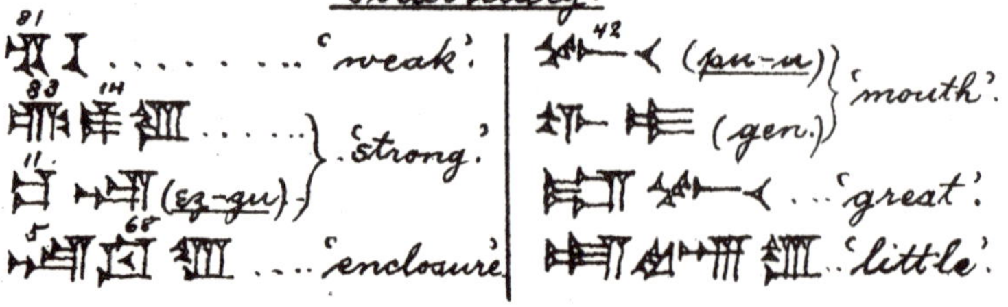

12 16,at ….. 'dagger.'

23 …. 'remainder.'

…. 'oath.'

or 88 …. " "

(or 75 ru) .. 'place.'

49 .. 'not accessible, inaccessible.'

38 …. 'lord.'

56 (qi) .. 'gift.'

95 .. 'the Urbi; a tribe.'

98 .. 'dwelling.'

53 (te) .. 'command.'

66 …… 'new.'

…. 'old.'

89 .. 'bright, shining.'

58, ti .. 'mud.'

ne 53 'a nêr = 600.

…. 'head.'

….. 'hand.'

58 .. 'anger.'

91(ap) …… 'son.'

…. 'woman.'

(see Lesson III. for the spelling).

.. 'high',

(gen. 31 ( )).

….. 'gate',

(gen.).

…. 'mountain.'

(gen.).

Lesson IX.

Exercise.

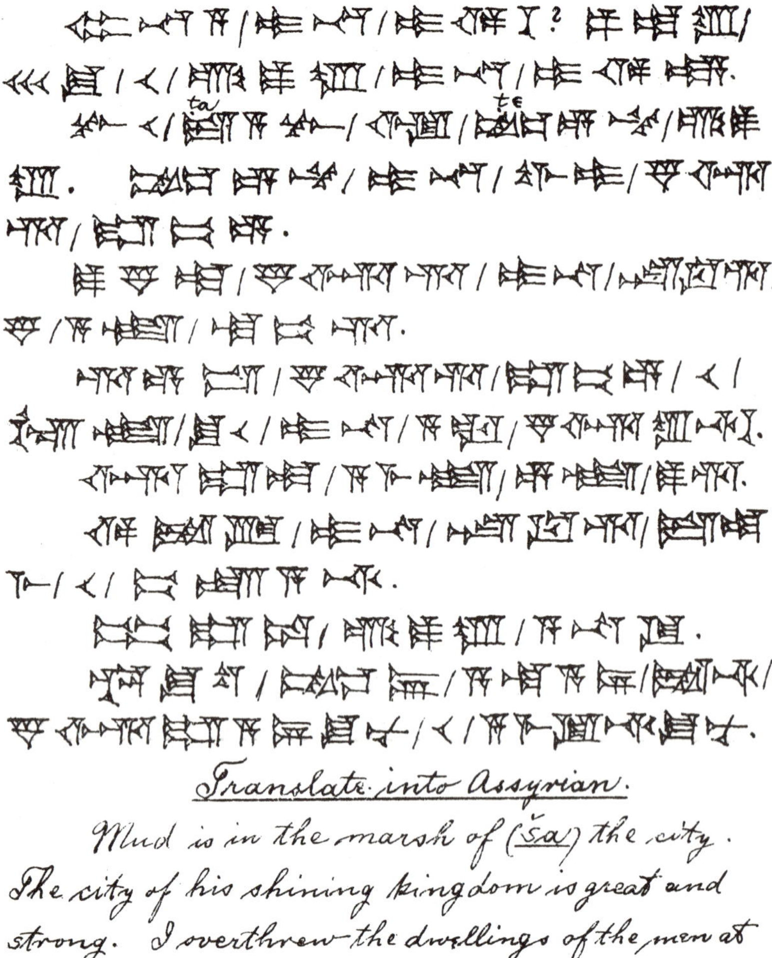

<u>Translate into Assyrian.</u>

Mud is in the marsh of (<u>ša</u>) the city. The city of his shining kingdom is great and strong. I overthrew the dwellings of the men at (<u>i-na</u>) the word (use <u>pu-u</u> 'mouth') of the king. With the great dagger in his hand he went in that road and looked at (<u>a-na</u>) the house of the great king. He is in the enclosure of the house. The ancient (old) gods of the shining city. Whose (who-his) hand is over me? The hand of the gods is over thee. My greeting to him and my curse to thee. The curse of the gods is over the city. I conquered those shining warriors who (were) with the princes and kings, in the inaccessible place. In anger I looked at (<u>a-na</u>) him. The son (<u>a-pi-il</u>) of the king gave it to you. The gate of the house is high. The god (is) lord of the high mountain.

Part II.

In the first part of this primer, to aid the beginner, the simple values have been presented in resemblance groups and not arranged according to the commonly accepted order.

In Part II, however, where the most common phonetic signs having compound values (as *bab*, *giš*) are given, this usual order has been observed, the principle of which must now be thoroughly understood by the learner; viz.,

1) Signs beginning with a single or reduplicated horizontal, 1–9.
2) With a single horizontal, in the centre of the sign, 10–29.
3) With a single horizontal at the bottom of the sign, 30–33.
4) With a single horizontal at the top of the sign, 34–35.
5) With two horizontals, 36–75.
6) With three horizontals, 76–83.
7) With four or more horizontals, 84–85.
8) With  and , 86–87.
9) With , 88–92.
10) With  and , 93–97.
11) With and , 98–102.
12) With , 103–119.
13) With , a single perpendicular, 120–121.
14) Square signs, 122–130.

15) With a perpendicular double at the bottom, 131 – 135.

16) With two perpendiculars, 136 – 138.

As in Part I. the new signs are all specified by number to facilitate their speedy identification. No sign given in Part I. is numbered in Part II., as the student must thoroughly have mastered Part I. before proceeding with the following lessons.

The ideographic system of writing, as its name denotes, used a number of single signs to represent certain words, as 𒀭 = <u>ilu</u> 'god'; 𒇽 = <u>a-me-lu</u> 'man', etc. These signs could be supplemented by what are called phonetic complements; i.e., phonetic simple symbols, indicating usually a grammatical ending. Thus: 𒀭 𒈨𒌍 𒉌 means that 𒀭 = <u>ilu</u> 'god' is plural as shown by 𒈨𒌍, the sign of the plural. The plural of <u>i-lu</u>, however, the student already knows to be <u>i-la-a-ni</u>, the ending of which <u>-ni</u> = 𒉌 was frequently written after the combination 𒀭 𒈨𒌍, as in the above example. The whole combination 𒀭 𒈨𒌍 𒉌, therefore, is read <u>i-la-a-ni</u>. In the same way, we find 𒌓 = <u>ûmu</u> 'day', written 𒌓 𒈬, 𒌓 𒈪 (gen.), etc., and 𒀭 followed by the vowel 𒂊 or 𒂊 is <u>always</u> to be read <u>šamû</u> or <u>šamê</u> 'heavens.'

The most commonly recurrent ideograms are given in the following lessons.

At this point the student must familiarize himself thoroughly with the verbal paradigm of kašâdu D. Gr. pp. 8ˣ–9ˣ. For one who has studied Hebrew, the mastering of this regular verb will be comparatively simple and may be done in a single lesson.

The other paradigms of the weak verbs (pp. 10ˣ–31ˣ) analogous to the similar verbs in Hebrew must then be read through at home, especial attention being paid to the verbs which are weak in the first consonant (pp. 12ˣ–16ˣ) and to the verb mediae ו and י (pp. 30ˣ–31ˣ).

With even a very general idea of the Assyrian verbal system the learner may proceed with the following graded readings, in which he will master all the common compound phonetic values of the signs and a number of the more usual ideograms. It is of course not intended that each lesson should be completed in one recitation. The time devoted to these readings will depend largely on the aptitude of the student and his knowledge of Hebrew or Arabic grammar. The greatest care must be taken not to read more at one time than can be easily assimilated.

Sign-List II.

Compound Phonetic Values.

No.	Values
1.	rum; dil, ṭil (see I. 75)
2.	ḫal.
3.	mug (k); (buk, puk).
4.	kus (š); rug (see I. 5).
5.	šun, šin; rug (k, g).
6.	bal, bul, (pal, pul).
7.	búl (púl)
8.	tar (ṭar); kut, gud, šil, ḫas (gug).
9.	nag (k, g).
10.	šaḫ, šiḫ.
11.	maḫ (miḫ).
12.	bab (pap); kur (gur).
13.	kat (d).
14	šub (p); see I. 97.
15.	bad (ṭ, t); mid (ṭ, t) til, tal, ziz. See I. 38.
16.	šir.
17.	kul, gul zir.
18.	bar (par); maš (s).
19.	kun, gun.
20.	pag (q); bag (k); see I. 45. Id. before or after word = "bird".
21.	nam (n); sim.
22.	mut (d).
23.	rat (ṭ, d).
24.	tal, dal (see I. 26).
25.	kab (p); gap; ḫup (b).
26.	tim, dim.
27.	mun.
28.	šur, sur.
29.	suḫ.
30.	kar (kan, gan).
31.	tik (q).
32.	tur, ṭur, dur.
33.	gur, kur.
34.	šak (q); riš (s). Ideogr. qaqqadu "head".
35.	dir, tir, ṭir.
36.	tab (p), ṭab, dab.

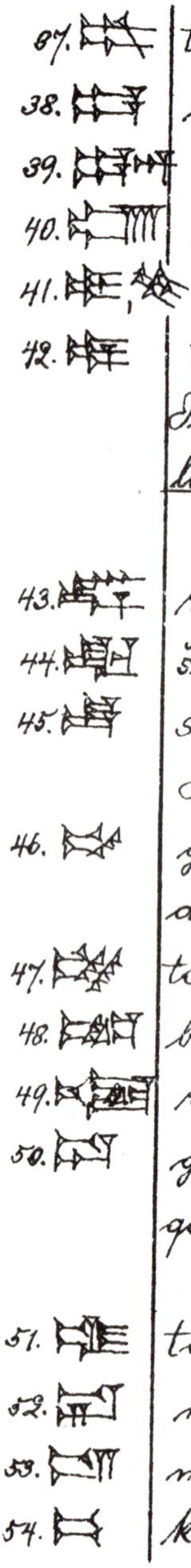

37. tak(q, g); šum.
38. nab(p).
39. mul.
40. dup.
41. , kan, gan (kam).
42. tur, ṭur, dur. Ideogr. *mâru*, *aplu* 'son'; *ṣiḫru* 'little'.
43. rab(p).
44. šar, sar, šir, ḫir
45. se, šum (see I. 86). Ideogr. *nadânu*
46. gab(p), qab, kab; daḫ, taḫ, duḫ, tuḫ.
47. taḫ, daḫ.
48. bil, pil (see I. 53);
49. ram.
50. gub (p), kub (p), qup, gin, kîn. (See I. 20.)
51. tum, dum (ib).
52. nit. See I. 21.
53. mil (see I. 22).
54. kaš(s), gaš (see I. 39).

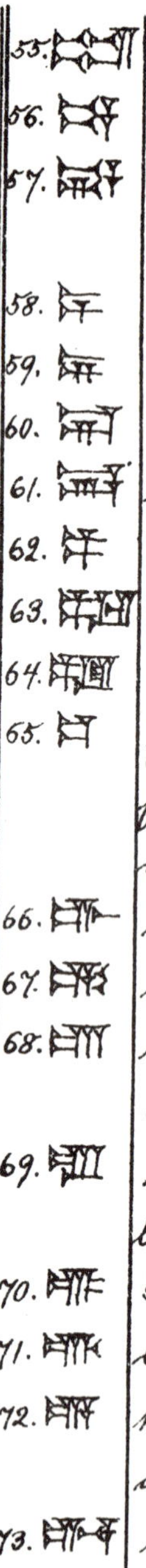

55. šim, rik(q).
56. kib(p), qib(p).
57. taq(k); dak. Ideogr. *abnu* 'stone'.
58. kak, qaq (dá).
59. zal, ṣal, : lí (see I. 8).
60. mal.
61. dak(q, g); tak, par.
62. had (ṭ, t). See I. 12.
63. šab(p), sap.
64. sib (p).
65. giš (see I. 11). Ideogr. for anything made of wood (see No. 129).
66. mar.
67. duk, lut (ṭ, d).
68. kit, qit, git; saḫ, siḫ, lil.
69. rit (d), šit (d), lak (q), mis (š, ṣ), (kil).
70. šam (see I. 82).
71. laḫ, liḫ, luḫ; (riḫ).
72. kal, rib, lab (p), (lib, p); dan, ṭan, tan.
73. ras.

74. bit (ṭ, d); pit; (é). Ideogr. bîtu 'house', [sign] = ekallu 'temple'.

75. nir, ner.

76. šiš (s), sis. Ideogr. aḫu 'brother'. Followed by [sign] = plural = aḫê 'brothers'.

77. zak (q).

78. kar, qar, gar.

79. lil.

80. gal, qal. Ideogr. for rabû 'great'.

81. biš, piš, puš; kir, gir.

82. mir.

83. bur, pur.

84. qat (d). See I. 59. Ideogr. qâtu 'hand'.

85. lul; lib (p); lup, pah, nar.

86. gam, qam, gur.

87. kur, mad (t); šad (t), lat, nat, kin, gin. Ideogr. for mâtu 'land' and when followed by a vowel -u or -i, -e for šadû 'mountain'.

88. sir, gid (t); qit (see I. 42).

89. šud (ṭ, t), sir.

90. ṣir, muš.

91. tir.

92. kar, gar.

93. liš (s).

94. tam, ṭam, par, pir, lah, lih, hiš (ṣ, s). See I. 72.

95. tal, ṭam. See I. 73.

96. ṣab (p); zab, bir, pir, lah, lih. Ideogr. ummanâti 'troops'.

97. lib in lib-bu 'heart'.

98. zib (p); sip.

99. sun. Ideogr. = plur.

100. bir, pir.

101. har, hir, hur; mur, kin.

102. huš; ruš.

103. muh. Ideogr. for prep. eli 'upon, against'.

104. lit (ṭ, d); rim.

105. kiš (s); qiš. Ideogr. [sign] [sign] = Kish.

106. gul, kul, qul; sun.

107. nim. Ideogr. Nim-ma-ki = Elam.

108. lam.

109. zur.

110. ban, pan.

111. kim, gim. Ideogr. for kîma 'like.'

112. lim (see I. 25). Ideogr. = abiktu 'defeat.'

113. ḫul.

114. tul. Ideogr. for tilu 'ruin, heap.'

115. din, tin.

116. dun; šul, sul.

117. pad (ṭ, t); šuk.

118. man, niš.

119. sin, zin (bá). See I. 66.

120. diš, ṭiš, tiz (š). Ideog. denoting masculine name.

121. lal (là).

122. kil, gil; rim (n); ḫab (p); pir.

123. zar, ṣar.

124. bul, pul.

125. zuk (q); suk.

126. šib (p); sib (p); see I. 73.

127. miš, meš. Ideogr. after nouns indicating the plural.

128. dur, tuš. See I. 56. = kakku 'weapon.' (see II. 66).

129. qin.

130. šik.

131. sal, šal; rak (g). Ideogr. mimma 'whatever, something.'

132. nin.

133. dam, tam.

134. niq (k).

135. lum (ḫum); (kus, gum).

136. tuk, tuq.

137. lik (q); taš (s); das, tiz, tiš, tes. See I. 33.

138. gug.

Lesson X.

Hymn to the Fire-god Bil-gi (H.T. 78-79).

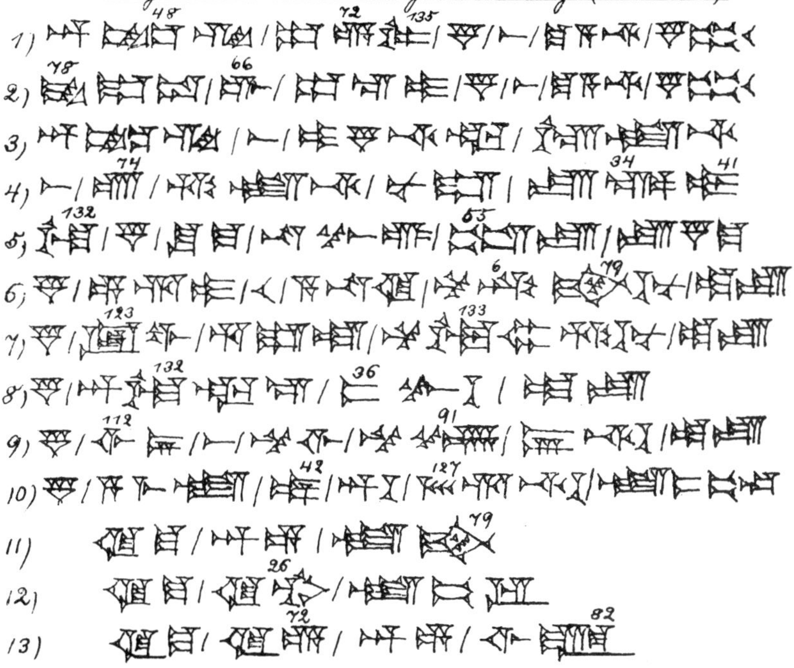

Note that the precative verbal prefix 3 p. is li-, as li-lil from alâlu = 'may he shine or be pure.'

Vocabulary.

1)  ... 'leader, mighty one'.

2)  ... 'warrior'; cf. קרד.

, constr.  .... } 'son'.
ideogr. 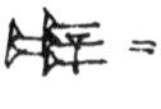 = 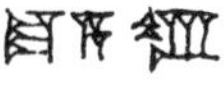, line 10.

 .... 'abyss'.

3) .... 'fire'.

, fem. of , q.v. Lesson IX.

4) = <u>bûtu</u> 'house'.

... 'darkness'.

.... 'light'

.... 'establish.'

5) , ideogr. for 'whatever, something'.

.... 'name'.

...... 'call, name.'

šim ..... 'fate', שים.

.... 'fix, establish', שים.

6) .... 'bronze'.

.... 'lead'; not to be confused with the word for 'I', Lesson I.

...... 'mix, fuse'.

7) (<u>sar-pu</u>) .. 'silver.'

...... 'gold'.

..... 'soften' (see Lesson XI).

8) (<u>tappu</u>) .. 'companion'.

9) .... 'evil'.

.... 'night'.

.... 'turn'. Where is <u>mutir</u> made? See Hollow verb (D. Gr. p 30× — 31×).

...... 'breast'.

10) ...... 'limbs'.

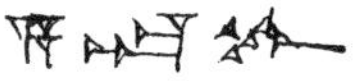

....'be pure, clean.' Used in I¹ and I²,  , ideogr. for *ilu* 'good,' but when followed by a vowel or  , ideogr. for *šamû, šamê* 'heavens'.

11)  ....'shine.'

12)  , ideogr. for *irṣitum* 'earth,' usually followed by the phonetic complement 51 or as here in the gen.  .

13) 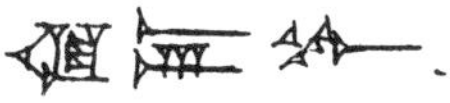 ....'midst.'

.... 'shine, be purified'; with the prec. prefix  , becomes *lim-mir* (= *lin-mir*).

Lesson XI.

Prism of Sennacherib (ALi⁴. 54).

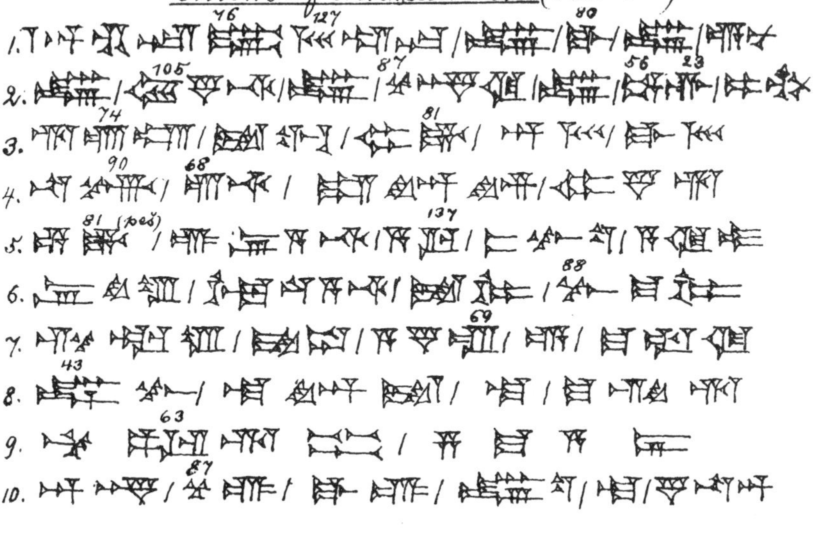

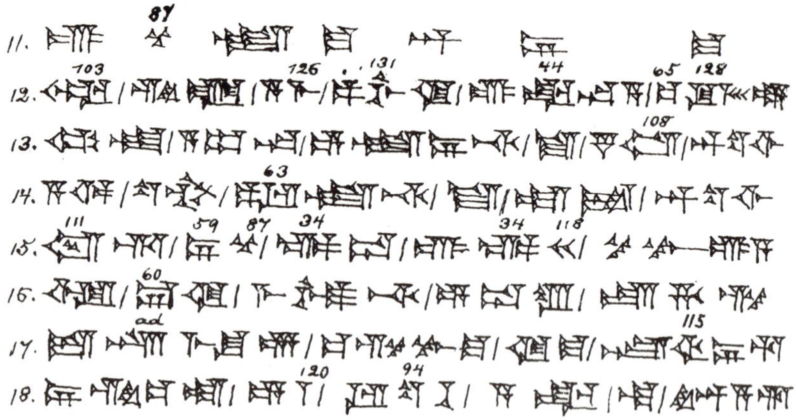

Learn the verb with the pronominal suffixes. | D. Gr., p. 32ˣ.

Vocabulary.

1.  indicates a man's name: here = Sin-aḫe-ir-ba = Sennacherib.

 indicates a god's name: here = Sin the moon-god.

 = ilu en-zu = The god Sin.

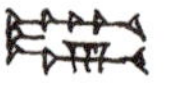 šiš - aḫu 'brother', followed by the plural sign  = aḫe.

 here has the phonetic value er + ba = erba from verb rabû 'increase' (see line 12). The whole name = Sin-aḫe-er-ba = 'Sin hath increased the brothers' and indicates that this king was not the first-born.

 : ideogr. for šarru 'king'.

 : ideogr. for rabû 'great'.

[cuneiform] from [cuneiform] = 'powerful'.

2) [cuneiform], gen. from stem [cuneiform] = universe, entirety?

[cuneiform], ideogr. for mâtu 'land' + [cuneiform] = Aššur 'Assyria'
+ [cuneiform] = ki postpositive indicating a place; not pronounced.

[cuneiform] = constr. fem. pl. of kib-ra-ti 'regions'.

[cuneiform], ideogr. for arba 'four' fem. irbittu + phon. fem. compl. -tim = irbit-tim.

3) [cuneiform] ri-e-um = rêu 'shepherd.'

[cuneiform] 'active' I^2 from stem [cuneiform].

[cuneiform] 'favourite'; [cuneiform]. See line 8.

[cuneiform] ilani pl. of ilu.

[cuneiform], pl. of [cuneiform] rabû = rabûti; why?

4) [cuneiform] (ša) 'protect'.

[cuneiform] ... 'justice.'

[cuneiform] ... 'love'? Verb mediae א 3

[cuneiform] ... 'righteousness'; from ישר.

5) [cuneiform] ... 'do, make'; א$_4$פש.

[cuneiform], from א$_1$סח = 'help, aid'.

[cuneiform] ... 'go'.

[cuneiform] (tap pu ut), cstr. of tappûtu 'assistance'.

[cuneiform] (adj.) = 'a crippled person.'

6) [cuneiform] 'surround; consider!'

[cuneiform] 'favourable'; damqâti 'favourable things.'

[cuneiform] 'hero'.

'perfect one', from .

How do you read here?

7) 'leader'. How is read here?

= kal 'all'.

8) , ptc. from שא$_2$ל 'destroy'.

'favourable, obedient.' See line 3.

9) 'lighten, thunder'. The Shaphel
= 'strike by lightning'.

za or ša ... 'foe'.

10. = šarru + ut, cstr. of šarrûtu 'kingdom'.

'vie with'; la ša-na-an = 'without equal.'

11) 'give, present.' What part of the verb? With what suffix?

12) , ideogr. for eli 'upon, against'.

... 'dwell'.

... 'royal chamber'; כדך.

, vb. final ה (י) = 'be great'.
Where is u-šar-ba-a made?

= kakku 'weapon'.

13) , ideogr. for tâmtu 'sea'. See line 14.

'upper' (fem.).

... 'setting' (of sun).

ilu Šamši, gen. of Šamaš 'sun-god', with phonetic complement -ši.

14) ... 'unto'.

 tâmtum 'sea' (see line 13).

 'lower' (fem.).

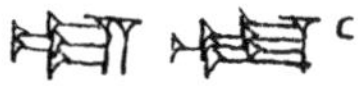 'rising' (of sun); from יצא = 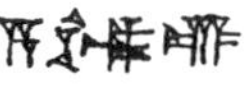
'go forth'.

15)  = sal-mat qaqqâdu 'the black ones of head' = 'the Babylonians'. Ṣalmu, fem. ṣalimtu, pl. ṣalmati = 'black'. Qaqqadu = 'head' = id. 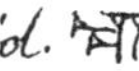 + , phon. complement.

 'bow down'; where is ušakniš made?

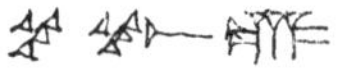 ..... 'foot'

16) 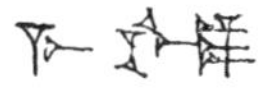 = šipṣu 'mighty'.

 .... 'fear'.

17)  ..... 'battle'; s.v. [illegible].

 ...'leave, abandon', = א$_4$זב. The suffix -ma after a verb is a pausal particle merely.

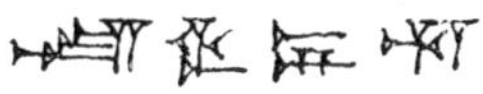 ... The Sudinnu bird (?).

18) , pl. = 'gorges'; see [illegible].

, adverb from  'one' = 'lonely'.

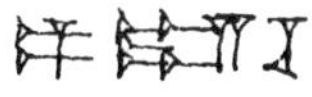 ..... 'flee.'

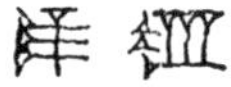 .... 'place'.

 .. 'inaccessible'. See Lesson VIII.
and s.v. [illegible].

Lesson XII, AL[4], p. 54, l. 19 ff.

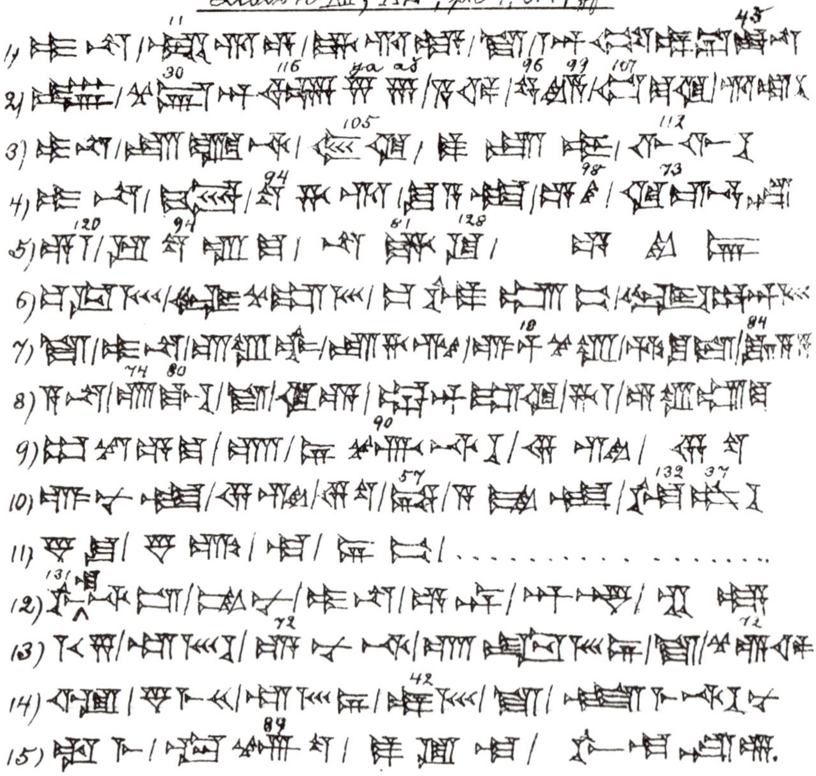

Vocabulary.

1) ... 'first'; מחר.

... 'campaign'; see s.v. ... = גרר.

... 'Marduk-apal-iddi-na',

= ... 'Marduk' + ... = aplu 'son' + ... = nadânu 'give' + phonetic complement -na = iddina. The name means: 'Marduk has given a son.'

2) The name Kar-dun-yaš was the Kassite term

for Babylon, the usual ideogram for which appears in line 8 of this selection.

[cuneiform], ideogr. for ṣâbu 'warrior'; in pl. denoted here by [cuneiform] (sun); the combination must be read ummanâti 'troops'; a fem. pl. of ummânu (q.v.)

[cuneiform] = Elâmtu = Elam with postpositive [cuneiform] of place.

[cuneiform] ([cuneiform]) = 'allies, helpers', from רצה.

3)  [cuneiform], with [cuneiform], means 'round about'; a prepositional phrase. See s.v. אטר.

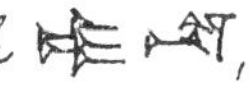

[cuneiform] = city of Kish, with postpositive [cuneiform] of place.

[cuneiform]. See s.v. שכן.

[cuneiform], ideogr. for abiktu 'defeat'; taḫtu 'overthrow'.

4)  [cuneiform], ideogr. for qablu 'midst'.

[cuneiform] (tam-ḫa-ru) 'battle'; see s.v. מחר.

[cuneiform]; see s.v. ארב₄.

[cuneiform] 'his camp' for ḳiraš-šu. See s.v. כרש.

5) 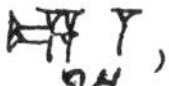 [cuneiform] (94), adv. from [cuneiform] 'one' = alone, lonely.

[cuneiform] (par-ša-du) 'flee'; a quadriliteral. See s.v. פרשד and פרש.

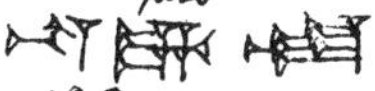

[cuneiform] (piš) 'life', with abbreviated suffix -š; [cuneiform] (129) = tuš here.

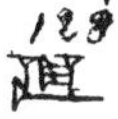

[cuneiform] (eṭeru) 'save'; see s.v. אטר₄.

6)  = *narkabâti*, pl. of *narkabtu* 'chariot'; i.e.,
, preformative for a wooden object +
 = *narkabtu* + 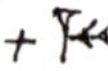 = plural.
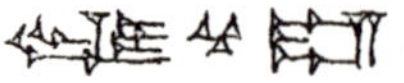 = *sîsu* 'horse'.
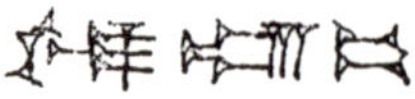 'draught-waggons', from צבב
for *ṣubbu* with inserted *m* to resolve
the doubling. Note the prefixed  here.
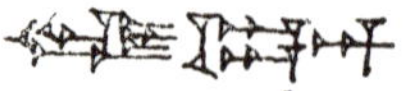 = *parû* 'mule'.

7)  'approach'; see s.v. קרב.
 .. 'battle'; see s.v. חוד.
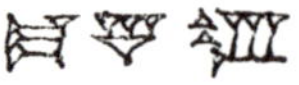 .. 'leave, depart'; see s.v. משר.
 .. 'conquer'; 3 p. pl. fem.; see s.v. כשד.
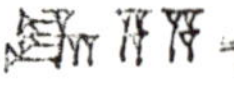 = *qatâ-ya* 'my hands'.  = ideogr. for
qâtu 'hand'. The two small perpendicu-
lars indicate a dual number, ending
in *-â*; i.e., *qatâ* +  here equivalent
to the 1 p. suffix . This is the first
instance of a dual thus far in the
lessons.

8) 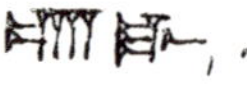, ideogr. for *ekallu* 'palace'.
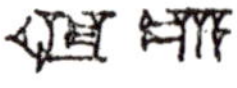, cstr. of  'midst'. See s.v.
קרב. Note that  = both *ki* and *qi*, to be
determined by the context and the reader's
knowledge of the stems.
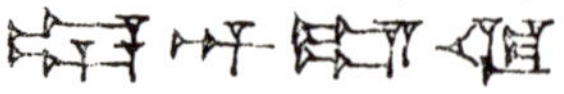 = *Bab-ilu* 'Babylon'; the
usual ideogram.

[cuneiform] 'joyfully'; adverb. See s.v. חדא.

[cuneiform] for e-ru-ub-ma 'I entered', the b of ערב being assimilated to the following m of the pausal particle [cuneiform]. The context demands the 1 p. here. See in D. Gr. 14× the paradigm of verbs primal א.

9) [cuneiform] 'I opened' from פתא. Note that a verb final ה (= ו or י) can always be known by the final overhanging vowel; here -e; aptê-ma.

[cuneiform] = bîtu 'house'.

[cuneiform] .. 'treasure'. See s.v. נצר.

[cuneiform], ideogr. for ḫurâṣu 'gold'; see s.v. חרץ.

[cuneiform], ideogr. for kaspu 'silver'.

10) [cuneiform] .. 'implements'; a collective abstract. (See s.v. אנא.)

[cuneiform] = abnu 'stone'; feminine.

[cuneiform] 'precious'; what gender? See s.v. יקר.

[cuneiform] = mimma 'whatever'.

[cuneiform] .. 'name'; see s.v. שם.

11) [cuneiform] = bušû 'property'; see s.v. בשה.

[cuneiform] = namkuru 'possessions'; see s.v. נכר.

[cuneiform] 'without number'; see s.v. מנא.

12) [cuneiform] 'as booty'; adverbial expression from šallâtu 'booty'. See s.v. שלל.

[cuneiform] 'I counted'; from מנא. Note again

the overhanging vowel denoting a verb final ה (= ו or י).

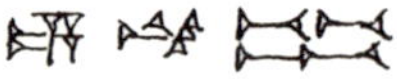

[cuneiform] 'power'; א$_4$מק.

[cuneiform] = the god <u>Ašur</u>.

[cuneiform] = <u>bêlu</u> 'lord'.

13)  [cuneiform] = the numerals 60 = [cuneiform] + 10 = [cuneiform] + 5 = [cuneiform] = 75.

[cuneiform] = <u>bît-durâni</u> (with supplementary <u>-ni</u>) 'fortresses'.

[cuneiform] = <u>mât Kaldi</u> 'Chaldaea'.

(14)  [cuneiform] = the numerals 4 = [cuneiform] + 100 = [cuneiform] + 20 = [cuneiform].

[cuneiform], ideogr. for <u>ṣiḫru</u> 'small' + pl. [cuneiform]. What is the proper pl. of mass. adjectives?

[cuneiform] 'border, boundary'. See s.v. למא$_2$.

15)  [cuneiform] 'I surrounded'; see s.v. למא$_2$.

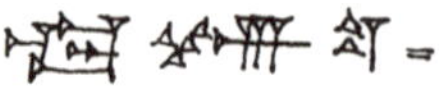

[cuneiform] = <u>ak-šud</u> (<u>ud</u>) 'I conquered'. The extra [cuneiform] = <u>ud</u> is added to fix the value of [cuneiform].

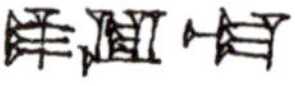

[cuneiform] 'I plundered'; see s.v. שלל.

[cuneiform] 'their booty' for <u>šallat-šun</u> from <u>šallâtu</u> (see above line 12). Whenever <u>t</u> + <u>š</u> come together, they change to <u>ss</u>.

Lesson XIII; AL⁴, 73, ℓ. 96 ff.

1) [cuneiform]
2) [cuneiform]
3) [cuneiform]
4) [cuneiform]
5) [cuneiform]

Selections from AL⁴, 70 (Esarh.).

6) [cuneiform]
7) [cuneiform]
8) [cuneiform]
9) [cuneiform]
10) [cuneiform]
11) [cuneiform]
12) [cuneiform]
13) [cuneiform]
14) [cuneiform]
15) [cuneiform]
16) [cuneiform]
17) [cuneiform]

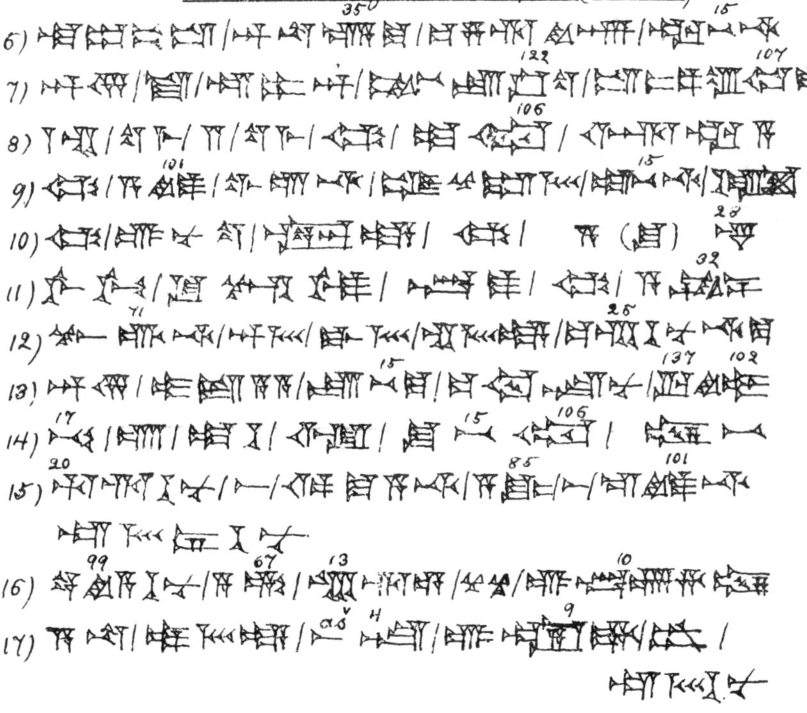

Vocabulary.

In the last three lessons only the stems of the words occurring in the lessons will be given, from which the student will be expected to read the forms in the reading-lessons.

1) [cuneiform], ideogr. for epru 'dust'; followed by [cuneiform] = pl..
[cuneiform], ideogr. for âlu 'city'; precedes city-names;
דוך whence maḍaktu 'fortification'.

2) חיד;

3) א$_4$רא$_2$; לקא$_3$; [cuneiform]; ideogr. = Aśur 'Assyria'.

4) זבל; זקר; שרף.

5) פוט; גמר; ספן.

6) לבא; נדר; צרח; כבת.

7) [cuneiform] = the goddess Ištar; [cuneiform] = City Arba-ili 'the four gods' = Arbela; [cuneiform], ideogr. = 'flesh', determinative here; תכל; שפר.

8) [cuneiform] = ištên 'one'; [cuneiform] = 'one' + [cuneiform] phon. complement; [cuneiform] ideogr. for ûmu 'day' + phon. compl. [cuneiform]; [cuneiform] = šina 'two'; דגל; ירך.

9) אמר; פקד; סיס; צמד; [cuneiform], ideogr. = nîru 'yoke', s.v. ניר.

10) אחז; [cuneiform], ideogr. = taḫâzu 'battle', s.v. חוד; אשר (note that [cuneiform] in this form is a prefixed complement; rare).

11) שלג; כצח; [cuneiform], ideogr. for arḫu 'month', s.v. ארח + [cuneiform] = the month Šabâṭu 'February-March'; אדר.

12) פלח; [cuneiform], ideogr. for bêlu 'lord', s.v. בא$_4$ל; סכף.

13) יד; נדד; [cuneiform], ideogr.: [cuneiform] determinative

for 'wood' + = *kaštu* 'bow'; שבר (note fem. *taš-bir*).

14) דרא₄; , ideogr. = *abu* 'father'; רשב; צבת.

15) סגר; דטא₄; אלל₁; סחר.

16) , ideogr.: = 'warrior' + = *ummanâti* 'troops'; דוד; כדר₁ אחד₁.

17) , ideogr. = *aplu*, *mâru* 'son'; שרק; נכר; שם.

Lesson XIV. Selections.

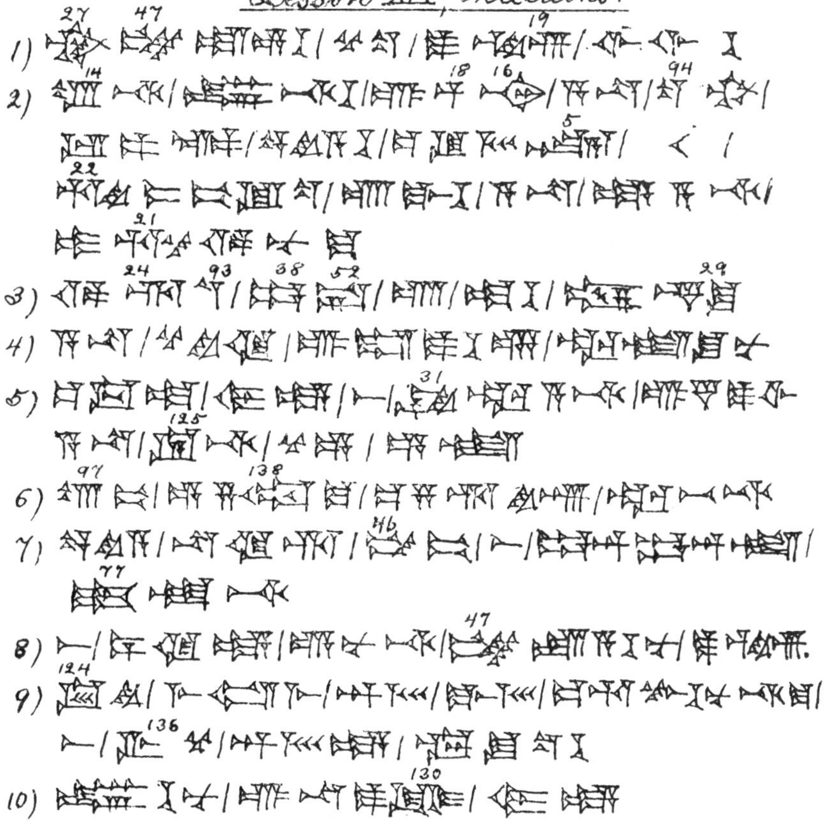

11) 12) 13)

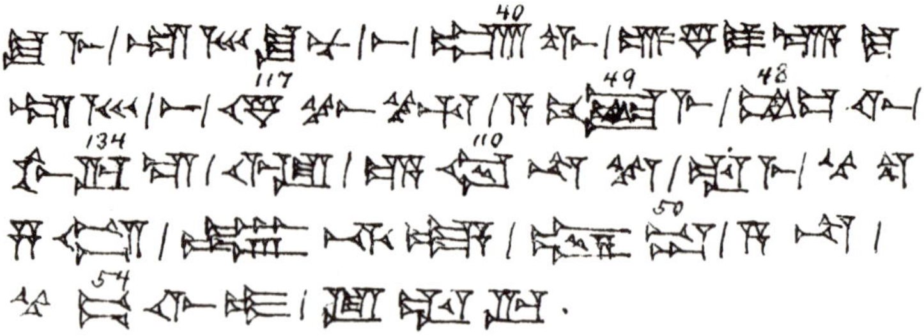

Vocabulary.

1) מחץ ; 𒆳 = *kašâdu* + complement 𒌓 = ud = *akšud* ; שכן.

2) ישב ; משר ; תא$_2$ם ; פרש ; זבל ; נדן.

3) ששל ; בוא$_2$; נסח.

4) זרי ; כול.

5) כרב ; שיך ; תכך ; נשא$_2$; זקת ; א$_4$לא$_2$.

6) לב ; אגג ; צרח ; כבת.

7) נכר ; גב ; מלמל ; זקת.

8) חתא$_2$; שכן.

9) פלח ; מלם ; [סחף ;] תכל ; כשד.

10) נשק.

11) שם ; דפף ; שטר.

12) כבט ; ארם ; פלש ; נכס ; כלבן ; למא$_2$; כשד.

13) צלם ; סקף ; א$_2$לך.

Lesson XV. Selections.

1)

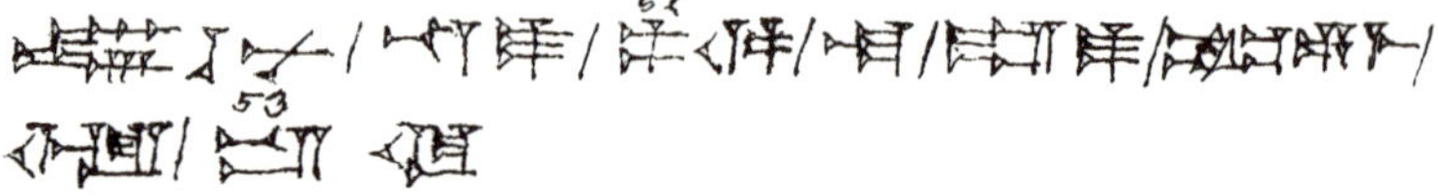

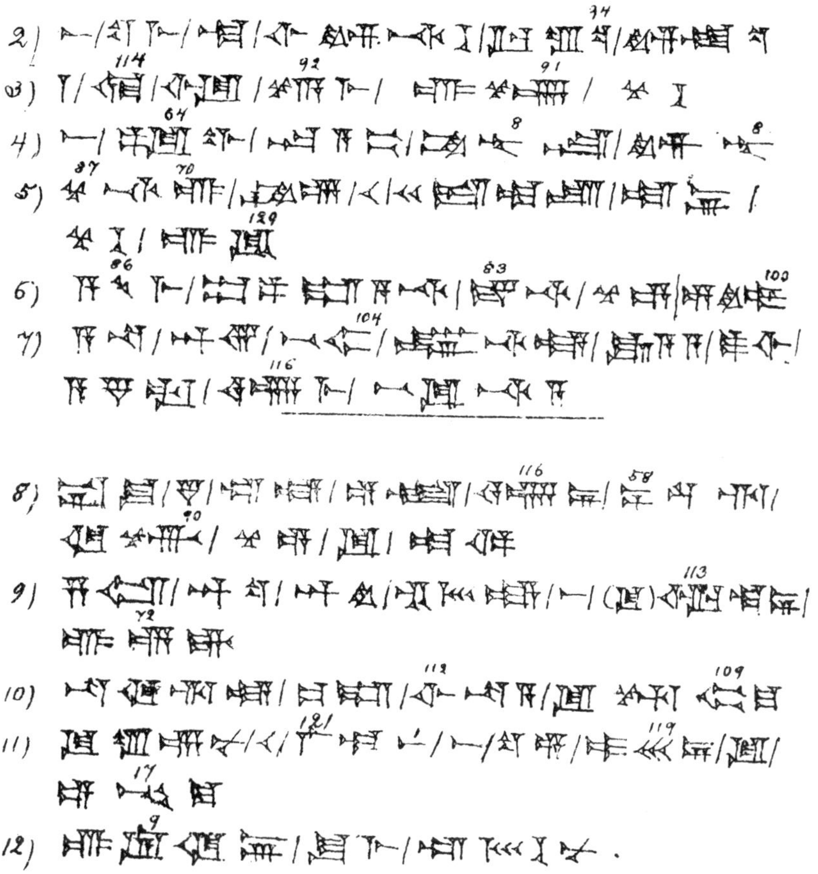

Vocabulary.

1) מלך; טא$_4$ם; רישא$_2$; חטט; בישא$_2$.

2) מות; ארח; שים.

3) אחד; כרם; חל.

4) מקת; מחץ; באב; ספף.

5) כון, ציר; נדן; רבל; שת.

6) א$_4$בר; בור; אפר; אגם.

7) בא$_4$ל; נשא$_2$; שא$_1$ל; שלם.

8) א$_1$שש; דגן; קקר; קצר; נדא$_2$.

9) צלם;  *is determinative for ṣubâtu 'garment', before garment-names as* *__ḫul-la-ai__*; *s.v.* חדל; לבש.

10) נכר; א$_4$זר; לטן; א$_4$זר.

11) כרן; ללר; א$_1$סן; א$_1$כל.

12) נכר.

Assyrian-English Glossary.

Note that in the following word-list, Arabic numerals standing alone refer to the pages of the preceding lessons and that small Roman numerals followed by Arabic numerals refer to the text of the last three lessons, the Arabic numerals indicating the numbered lines. Thus, 48 would mean page 48, but XV, 10 indicates the tenth line of the fifteenth lesson.

Note also that verbs final א$_2$ are indicated throughout by final ה.

א

אא$_3$ד *êdu* 'one', 11; *êdiš* 'alone', 39, 41.

אא$_2$ל *âlu* 'city', pl. *alâni*, 15.

אב *abu* 'father', pl. *abûti*, 8; *abišu* 'his father', (gen.), XIII, 14.

אבב *abâbu* 'shine, be pure', 35; prec. *libbib* 'may he shine'; adj. *ebbu* 'shining, pure'.

אבך *abiktu* 'defeat'; ideogr. ŠI—ŠI, 41.

אבכל *abkallum* 'leader, governor', 33.

אבן *abnu* 'stone', 43.

א$_4$בר *ebêru* 'cross over', 49; pret. *êbir*, XV, 6.

אגג *agâgu* 'be angry'; pret. *egugma*, XIV, 6. Noun: *uggatu* 'anger', 23.

אגם *agammu* 'marsh', 49; pl. *agamme*, XV, 6.

א$_4$ד *adi* prep. 'unto, as far as, together with', 38.

אדר *adâru* 'fear', 39; pret. *adur*, XII, 11.

א$_3$דשׁ *eššu* 'new', 23.

א$_4$זב *ezêbu* 'leave, abandon', 39, 41.

א$_4$זז *ezzu* 'strong, powerful', 22.

א$_4$זר *ezêru* 'curse'; prec. pret. 1 p. *luzzurma*, XV, 10; *ezru* 'a curse', XV, 10.

אח *aḫu* 'brother', 15; *aḫatu* 'sister', 15.

אחז *aḫâzu* 'seize, grasp', 47; III, 1 *ušaḫḫaz*, XIII, 16.

א$_4$טר *eṭêru* 'spare, save', 41.

א$_4$ין *ênu* 'eye', 11.

איר *âru* 'reach, attain', 23, 39.

אכה *akû* 'cripple, feeble', 37.

אכל *akâlu* 'eat'; pret. *ekulma*, XV, 11.

אכל* *ekallu* 'temple, palace', 42. Not a Semitic word, but from Sumerian *e-gal* 'big house'.

אל *ilu* 'god', pl. *ilâni*, 11, 37.
אל *ul* 'not'; usual negative = Heb. לא.
אל* *ultu* prep. 'from', 11.
אלה$_4$ *elû* 'go up, ascend', 48; pret. *elî*, XIV, 5. Adj. *elinû*, fem. *elinîtu* 'upper', 38. Prep. *eli* 'against, over', 11.
אלך$_2$ *alâku* 'go', 37, 48; pret. 1 p. *allik*, XIV, 13; 3 p. *illik*, 19.
אלל *alâlu* 'shine, be bright', 35; adj. *ellu*, fem. *ellîtu* 'bright, pure', 23, 34.
אלל *alâlu* 'hang' (trans.); pret. 1 p. *alul*, XIII, 15.
אם *ummu* 'mother', 15.
אם$_3$ *emû* 'father-in-law'; *emêtu* 'mother-in-law', 15.
אמל *amêlu* 'man'; pl. *amelûti*, 11.
אמן *ummanâti* 'troops', 41; XIII, 16.
אמק *emûqu* 'power', 44.
אמר *amâru* 'see'; pret. 1 p. *amur*, XII, 9.
אמר *tamirtu* 'circumference'; *ina tamirti* 'around', 41.
אמר$_3$ *imêru* 'ass', 15.
אן *ana* prep. 'unto': *ina* 'in, by', 11.
אנה *annû* 'this'; fem. *annîtu*, 19; pl. *annûtu* (*ti*), *annâti*, 20.
אנו *unûtu* 'furniture, implements', 43; XII, 10.
אנך *anâku* pron. 1 p. 'I', 8.
אנּך *anâku* 'lead' (metal), 34.
אנן *anînu* 'we'; also: *anîni*, *nênu*, *nîni*, 8.
אנש *enšu* 'weak', 22.
אסה *usâti* 'help, assistance', 37.
אסן *isinnu* 'feast', 50; *isinni*, XV, 11.
אפל *aplu* 'son', 23.
אפס *apsû* 'abyss, ocean', 33.
אפש$_4$ *epêšu* 'do, make', 37; adj. *itpišu* 'active, capable'.
אפר *apâru*: *apparâti* pl. of *apparu* 'marsh', 45; XV, 6.
אפר$_4$ *epru* 'dust', 46.
אר *irtu* 'breast, front', 34.
ארב$_4$ *Urbi*; name of a tribe, 23.
ארבא$_4$ *irba* 'four', 37.
ארה$_4$ *eriš* 'like an eagle', XII, 3 from *erû* 'eagle', 34.
ארח *urḫu* 'road', 19; XII, 11; XV, 2.
ארם *aramme*, pl. 'siege instuments', 48; XIV, 12.
ארץ *irṣitu* 'earth', 11.
ארר *arâru* 'curse'; *arratu* 'a curse', 23.
אש* *ištu* prep. 'from', 11.
אש *išatu* 'fire', 34.
אשר *ašâru* 'care for, pay attention to'; pret. *ašur*, XII, 10.
אשר *ašru* 'place', 23, 39.
אשרד *ašâridu* 'leader', 38.
אשש *uššu* 'foundation', 11; XV, 8.
אשת *aššatu* 'wife, woman', 11, 23.
אשתן$_4$ *ištên* 'one', XII, 8.
את *itti* 'with', 11.
אתה *atta* 'thou', fem. *atti*, 8; *attûnu* 'ye', 8.
אתל *itlum* 'hero'; sometimes written *idlum*, 37.

ב

באב *bâbu* 'gate', 23, 49; XV, 4.
בא$_4$ל *bêlum* 'lord', 23, 44; XII, 12; *bêlit*, constr. of *bêltu* 'lady', 50; XV, 7.
בור *bûrtu* 'well', 49; XV, 6.
בית *bîtu* 'house', 11, 34, 43. *Bîtdûrani* 'fortifications', 44.
במה *bamâte(ti)* 'high-places, heights', 15.
בנה *banû* 'build, beget'; noun: *nabnîtu* 'offspring', XIV, 3.
ברק *barâqu* 'lighten', 38.
בשׁה *bašû* 'be, exist', 11; *bušu* 'property', 43.

ג

גב *gabbu* 'all', XIV, 7.
גמל *gitmalum* 'perfect', 38.
גמר *gimru* 'entirety', constr. *gimir*, 19; XII, 5.
גרר *garâru* 'run'; *girru* 'campaign', 40.
גשׁר *gašru* 'mighty', 22.

ד

דגל *dagâlu* 'look'; pret. *adgul*, XII, 8; *idgul*, 19.
דדם *dadmu* 'dwelling'; pl. *dadme*, 23.
דוך *dâku* 'slay, kill'; pret. *adûk*, XIII, 16; *madâktu* 'fortification'.
דמא$_4$ *dimâti* 'posts, stakes', XII, 15; pl. of *dimtu*.
דמק *damâqu* 'be favourable to', 34; adj. *damqu* 'favourable, gracious', 37.
דנן *danânu* 'be powerful'; adj. *dannu* 'powerful', 15, 37; fem. *dannatu*, 15. Noun: *dunnu* 'power, strength', XV, 8.
דפף *duppu* 'clay tablet', XIV, 11.

ו

ו *u* 'and', 11.
ובל *abâlu* 'carry, bring'; nouns: *muttabilûtu* I, 2 partc. 'portable things'; *biltu* 'tribute', 49; XV, 5.
וצא *aṣû* 'go out'; noun: *ṣîtu* 'rising of the sun', 39.
ורה *arû* 'bring'; *uraššu*. XIV, 4 = *urâ* + *šu*.
ורך *arkû* 'after', XII, 8.
ושׁב *ašâbu* 'dwell' 38; noun: *šubtu* 'dwelling', XIV, 2; with suffix *šubatsun*, XIII, 14.

ז

זכר *zikaru* 'hero, male', 11.
זמן *zamânu* 'enemy', 38.
זקף *zaqâpu* 'set up'; *azqup*, XIV, 13.
זקת *zaqâtu* 'be sharp'; *zaqtu*, pl. *zaqtûti* 'sharp', XIV, 7. Noun: *zuqtu* 'sharp peak', XIV, 5.
זרא$_4$ *zêru*: constr. *zêr* 'seed', XIII, 14.

ח

חדה *hadiš* 'joyfully', 43.
חזז *taḫazu* 'battle', 39, 42; XII, 10. *Maḫazu* 'city', XII, 2.
חטט *ḫaṭṭu* 'sceptre', XV, 1.
חל *ḫullanu* 'garment', XV, 9.
חרץ *ḫurâṣu* 'gold', 34, 43.
חתה *taḫtû* 'defeat': *taḫtâšunu*, XIV, 8.

ט

טא₄ם *ṭêmu* 'counsel, wisdom, taste', XV, 1.
טוב *ṭâbu*, fem. *ṭâbtu* 'good', 15.
טוד *ṭûdu* 'road', 19.
טיט *ṭîṭu* 'clay, mud', 23.
טטל *ṭiṭallu* 'torch'; *ṭiṭalliš*, 'like a torch', XIV, 3.

י

יאת *iâti* 'me', 13.
יד *idu* 'hand', 23; *idâ-ia* 'my hends', (dual), XII, 13.
יקר *aqartu*, fem. 'precious', 43.
ישר *mišaru* 'righteousness', 37.

ך

ך *kâša* 'thee'; *kâši*, 13; *kâšunu* 'you', 13.
כבס *kabâsu* 'tread', III, 1, partc. constr.; *šukbus* 'hostile advance', XIV, 12.
כבר *kibrâti* 'regions', 37.
כבת *kabittu* 'heart, liver', XIV, 6.
כדר *kadre* 'gifts, tribute', 47; XIII, 16.
כול *kâlu* 'all', 38; *kâlišunu* 'all of them', XIV, 4.
כון *kânu* 'establish', 49; pret. *ukîn*, XV, 5. Noun: *kittu* 'righteousness', 37.
כי *kîma* 'like, like to', 11.
כך *kakku* 'weapon', 38.
ככבן *kalbannâti* 'axes', 48; XIV, 12.
כנש *kanâšu* 'bow down', 39.
כסף *kaspu* 'silver', 43.
כצה *kuṣṣû* 'cold', XII, 11.
כרם *karmu* 'ploughed field', XV, 3.
כרן *kurunnu* 'wine', XV, 11.
כרש *kirâšu* 'camp'; with suffix *kirassu*, 41.
כשד *kašâdu* 'conquer'; pret. 1 p. *akšud*, 19, XIV, 9, 12, 44; *ikšudâ*, 3 pl. fem., 42.
כשש *kiššâti* 'hosts', 37.

ל

לא *lâ* 'not', 11.

לא$_4$ט partc. *lâ*, *iṭ* 'swallow up, devour', 38.

לב *libbu* 'heart'; *libbi*, XIV, 6.

לבר *labîru* 'old, ancient', 23.

לבשׁ *labâšu* 'be clothed; II, 1 *ulabbiš*, XV, 9.

לו *lû* 'verily', 11. Strengthening and precative particle.

לושׁ *lišânu* 'tongue, language', 15.

ללר *lallarum* 'honey', XV, 11.

למה *lamû* 'surround'; pret. 1 p. *almî*, XVI, 12. Noun: *limêtu* 'boundary, border', 44.

למן *limnu* 'evil', 34; XV, 10.

לקא$_3$ *liqû* 'take'; pret. *alqâ*, XII, 3.

מ

מא$_2$ר *mâru* 'son', 33.

מאם *mimma* 'whatever, something', 34, 43.

מאת *mâtu* 'land', 15. Probably not a Semitic word, but from Sumerian *mada*.

מגר *magâru* 'favour', 38; *migru*, constr. *migir* 'favourite', 37.

מות *mâtu* 'die'; I, 2. *imtût*, XV, 2.

מחץ *maḫâṣu* 'smash, smite'; pret with suffix: *amḫaṣṣu* 'I smote him'. Noun: *mundaḫṣu* 'warrior', for *mumtaḫiṣu*.

מחר *maḫru* 'first', 40; *tamḫâru* 'battle', 41.

מכר *namkuru* 'property', 43.

מלא *malû* 'be full'; *mala* 'as many as', 11.

מלך *malâku* 'rule, counsel'; *mâliku*, pl. *malke*, *malkâni* 'prince'; *malkatu*, pl. *malkâti* 'princess', 15; *milku* 'counsel, advice' XV, 1.

מן *mannu* 'who?'; *minû* 'what?', 20.

מנה *manû* 'count, reckon'; pret. *amnû*, 43.

מקת *maqâtu* 'fall'; pret. *amqut*, 49.

משׁ *mušu* 'night', 34.

משׁר *mašâru* 'leave, abandon; II, 1, *umaššir* 'he left', XIV, 2.

משׁר *mešrîti* 'limbs', 34 (?).

נ

נבא *nabû* 'speak, utter', 34; *nibu* 'number', 45.

נבל *nabâlu* 'destroy'; pret. *abul*, XII, 4.

נגץ *nigiṣṣu* 'gorge', 39.

נדה *nadû* 'set, place, lay'; pret. *addi*, XV, 8.

נדן *nadânu* 'give'; pret. *iddin*, 15; pres. 3 pl *inamdinû-ma*, XIV, 2. Noun: *mandatu* 'tribute, gift', XV, 5.

נור *nûru* 'light', 34.

נזז *nazâzu* 'stand'; pret. 3 p. fem. *tazziz-ma*, XII, 13; 1 p. *azzaz*, 19.

ניאת *niâti* 'us', 13.

ניר *nîru* 'yoke', XII, 9.

ניר *nêru* 'a ner' = 600.

נכס *niksu* 'breach in a wall', XIV, 12.
נכר *nakâru* 'change, hostile'; II, 1, *unakkir*, XIII, 16; XV, 12.
Noun: *nâkiru* 'enemy', XIV, 7; XV, 10.
נמר *namâru* 'shine', 35.
נסח *nasâḫu* 'tear away'; pret. *assuḫ*, XIV, 3.
נפשׁ *napištu* 'life', 41.
נצר *naṣâru* 'keep', 37. Noun: *niṣirtu* 'treasure', 43.
נקר *naqâru* 'tear down, destroy'; pret. 1 p. *aqur*, XII, 4.
נשׂא *našû* 'lift up'; pret. 1 p. *aššî*, XV, 7: III, 1, *ušaššî* with fem. suffix, XIV, 5; partc. *nâš*, XV, 1.
נשׁק *našâqu* 'kiss'; II, 1. *unaššiq*, XIV, 10.

ס

סדן *sudinnu* 'a sort of bird', 39.
סחף *saḫâpu* 'overthrow'; pret. *isḫup*, XIV, 9.
סחר *saḫâru* 'surround', 37; *ina siḫirti*: prep. 'around', XIII, 5.
סיס *sîsu* 'horse, 42; XII, 9.
סכף *sakâpu* 'overthrow'; pret. *askup*, 19; *iskap*, XII, 12.
סמן *samnu*, ordinal: 'eighth', 11.
ספן *sapânu* 'sweep away, overthrow'; *aspun*, XII, 5.
ספף *sippu* 'threshold', 49; XV, 4.
ספר *supûru* 'enclosure', 22.
סת *sittu*, pl. *sittûti* 'rest, remainder', 23.

פ

פגר *pagru* 'corpse'; *pagriš* 'like a corpse', XIII, 15.
פו *pû*, gen. *pî* 'mouth', 22.
פוט *pâṭu* 'limit', XII, 5: *pâṭ gimri* 'entirety'.
פטר *paṭâru* 'split'; Noun: *paṭru* 'dagger', 23.
פלח *palâḫu* 'fear'; *pulḫu*, XIV, 9; *puluḫtu* 'fear', XII, 12.
פלשׁ *pilšu*, pl. *pilši(e)* 'hole, mine', 48; XIV, 12.
פקד *piqittu* 'order, muster', XII, 9.
פר *paru* 'mule', 42.
פרך *parakku* 'royal chamber, shrine', 38.
פרשׁ *parâšu* 'flee', 39; IV, 1, pret. *ippariš* XIV, 2.
פרשׁד *paršâdu* 'flee', 41. Quadriliteral from פרשׁ.
פתא$_3$ *pitû* 'open'; pret. *aptê-ma*, 43.

צ

צבא *ṣâbu* 'warrior', 41.
צבב *ṣumbu* 'cart'; pl. *ṣumbe*, 42.
צבת *ṣabâtu* 'seize'; pret. 1 p. *aṣbat*, XIII, 11.
צחר *ṣiḫru* 'little, small', 22, 44.
ציר *ṣîru*, constr. *ṣîr* 'against', XV, 5.
צלם *ṣalmu* 'image'; constr. *ṣalam*, 19; XIV, 12; XV, 9.

צלם *ṣalmu* 'black'; fem. pl. constr. *ṣalmât*: *ṣalmât qaqqadi* 'the black headed ones', i. e., the Babylonians, 39.
צמד *ṣimittu* 'span, team', XII, 9.
צצה *ṣuṣû* 'marsh', 19.
צרח *ṣarâḫu* 'cry out'; I, 2. *iṣṣariḫ*, XII, 6; XIV, 6.
צרף *ṣarpu* 'refined silver', 34.

ק

קאת *qâtu* 'hand', 19; dual *qatâ*, 42.
קבל *qablu* 'midst; combat', 41.
קיש *qîštu* 'gift', 23.
קצר *qiṣru* 'strength, power'; constr. *qiṣir*, XV, 8.
קקד *qaqqadû* 'head', 39.
קקר *qaqqâru* 'territory, ground', XV, 8.
קרב *qirbu* midst', 35; constr. *qirib*, 42; *qitrubu* 'battle, attack', 42.
קרד *qarradu* 'warrior', 33; *qurâdu* 'warrior', 15.
קשת *qaštu* 'bow'; *qašâtsunu* 'their bows', XII, 13. Pl. is *qašâti*.

ר

$ר א_4 ה$ *rêum* 'shepherd', 37.
$ר א_3 ם$ *râmu* 'love', 37.
ראש *rêšu* 'head', 15, 23.
רבה *rabû* 'be big, large'; III, 1. *ušarbâ*, 38. Adj. *rabû*, fem. *rabîtu*, pl. *rabûti*, *rabâti* 'big, large', 22, 37.
רכב *rakâbu* 'ride, mount'; noun: *narkabtu*, constr. *narkabat*; pl. *narkabâti*, XIV, 5.
רצה *raṣû* 'help, aid'; pl. partc. *riṣê* 'allies', 41.
רשה *rašû* 'possess'; used particularly of mental qualities; partc. seen in *râš ṭêmi* 'possessor of counsel, understanding', XV, 1.

ש

ש *ša*: rel. pron. 'who'; prep. 'of', 11, 19.
שאל *ša'âlu* 'ask'; pret. 1 p. *ašâl*, XV, 7.
$ש א_3 ר$ *šêru* 'morning', 15.
שבר *šabâru* 'break'; pret. 3 p. fem. *tašbir*, XII, 13.
שדה *šadû* 'mountain', 23.
שו *šû* 'he; that one', 8. *Šî* 'she', 8. *Šunu*, *šina* 'they' (masc. and fem.). *Šâšu*, fem. *šâši*, 8, 13; *šuatu*, fem. *šiati*, pl. *šuatunu*, fem. *šiatina*, 19; also *šatunu*, masc. pl. demonstrative pronoun = 'that one, those ones'.
שטר *šaṭâru* 'write'; III, 1. *ušašṭir-ma*, XIV, 11.
שים *šâmu* 'set, fix, establish'; *šîmtu* 'fate, destiny', 34; XV, 2.
שיף *šêpu* 'foot', 48; *šêpi-ia* 'my feet', XIV, 5.
שכן *šakânu* 'set, establish', 34; pret. *aškun*, XIV, 8; I, 1. *aštakan*, 41.
שלג *šalgu* 'snow', XII, 11.

שלל *šalâlu* 'take as booty'; pret. *ašlula*, 44. Noun: *šallatu* 'booty': *šallatiš* 'as booty', 43; *šallasunu* = *šallat-šunu* 'their booty', 44.
שלם *šalâmu* 'set' (of the sun), 38. Noun: *šulmu* 'peace, greeting', 19, 50; XV, 7.
שם *šumu* 'name', 34, 43; pl. *šume*, XIV, 11; constr. sing. *šum*, XIII, 16.
שמה *šamû* 'heaven'; pl. *šamê*, 35.
שנה *šinâ* 'two', XII, 8.
שנן *šanânu* 'rival, vie with', 38.
שפל *šaplu*, fem. *šaplîtu* 'low', 39.
שפץ *šipṣu* 'might, power', 39.
שפר *šipru* 'message'; constr. *šipir*, 19.
שר *šarru*, pl. *šarrâni* 'king', 15; *šarrûtu* 'kingdom, royalty', 38.
שרף *šarâpu* 'burn'; pret. 1 p. *ašrup*, XII, 4.
שרק *šarâqu* 'give'; pret. 1 p. *ašruq*, XIII, 16.
שקה *šaqû* 'high', 23.
שת *šattu* 'year', 49; *šattišam* 'annually', XV, 5.

ת

תא₂ם *tâmtu(m)* 'sea', 38, 39; gen. *tâmtim*, XIV, 2.
תור *târu* 'turn, return', 34; III, 1. *utîr*, XV, 3.
תכך *tikkâti* 'ropes', XIV, 5.
תכל *tukultu*, constr. *tuklat* 'trust, confidence', XIV, 9.
תל *tilu* 'hill, mound', XV, 3.
תלם *talâmu* 'give, present', 38.
תף *tappu* 'companion', 34; *tappûtu* 'companionship', 37. This is probably from Sumerian *tab* 'two' and is consequently non-Semitic.

CORRIGENDA TO THE LESSONS

Page 33. In Lesson X, line 2, the RA-sign should have an extra perpendicular wedge.

Page 35. Vocabulary, line 10, for "good," read "god."

Page 45. In Lesson XIII, line 13, the sign BIR should be numbered 100 and not 102.

Page 48. Vocabulary, line 13, read זכה for סכף.

Page 49. Vocabulary, line 3, read תור for אחז.

CORRIGENDA AND ADDENDA TO THE GLOSSARY, pp. 51–58

In the Glossary, all roots referred from the Vocabulary of Lesson XIII, lines 2–13, incl., should have the reference XIII, instead of XII.

ארח Add *arḫu* 'month,' XIII, 11; *urruḥiš* 'quickly,' XV, 2.

אכל$_3$ Add *eklîtu* 'darkness,' X, 4.

ארה$_2$ Add *erû* 'bronze,' X, 6.

באל$_4$ Add *bêlûtu* 'dominion,' XV, 7.

בלל Add participle *mubaliil* 'fusing,' X, 6.

כבת Read XIII, 6; XIV, 6.

כשר Read 19, 44; XIV, 9, 12.

לבא Add *labbiš* 'like a lion,' XIII, 6.

לכה For XVI, 12, read XIV, 12.

כלם Add *melammu* 'splendor,' XIV, 9.

כלכל Add *mulmullu* 'javelin,' XIV, 7.

מקת Add *imqut*, XV, 4.

נדר Add *annadirma* 'I raged,' IV, 1; XIII, 6.

סחר For XIII, 5, read XIII, 15.

פגר Omit *pagriš* 'like a corpse,' XIII, 15.

צבת For XIII, 11, read XIII, 14.

צלם For XIV, 12, read XIV, 13.

שכן Add pret. *aškun*, XIV, 1, 8; Ifteal *aštakan*, 41.

שפר Add Ifteal *ištapparûnimma* 'they sent me,' XIII, 7.

תכל Add *takiltu* 'oracle,' XIII, 7.

Assyrian king in battle. Nimroud.

Battle-scene. Nimroud.

Siege. Nimroud.

ARCHAIC CLASSICS.

ASSYRIAN TEXTS.

Winged figure. From a gate at Nimroud.

ARCHAIC CLASSICS.

ASSYRIAN TEXTS

BEING

EXTRACTS FROM THE ANNALS OF SHALMANESER II., SENNACHERIB, AND ASSUR-BANI-PAL.

With Philological Notes

BY

ERNEST A. BUDGE, M.R.A.S.
ASSYRIAN EXHIBITIONER, CHRIST'S COLLEGE, CAMBRIDGE.

LONDON:
TRÜBNER AND CO., LUDGATE HILL.
SAMUEL BAGSTER AND SONS, PATERNOSTER ROW.
1880.

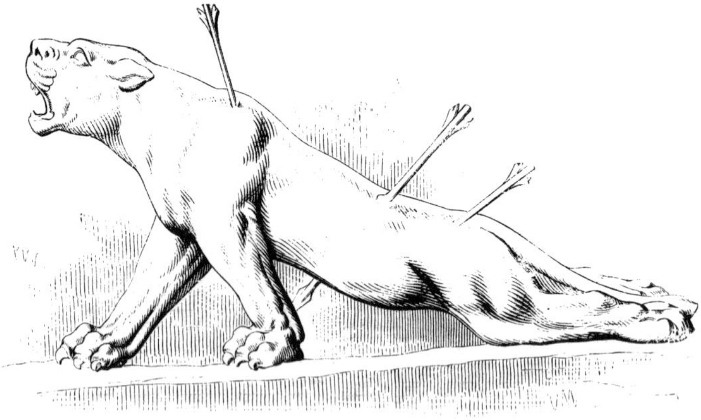

Dying lioness. Relief from Kouyunjik.

PREFACE.

THE want of a selection of Assyrian texts in the form of a Reading Book has been felt and often expressed by Students, the more so on account of many of the Assyrian books that have been published in England being out of print. This selection (which is based upon the proposals made by Mr. Boscawen to Messrs. Bagster) has been made to include specimens of the best historical texts, and these have been annotated in a similar manner to the valuable pages in Prof. Sayce's *Assyrian Grammar*. Each character has been carefully compared with the original texts preserved in the British Museum, and it is therefore hoped that they will be found free from error. My thanks are due to Mr. Pinches for his kindness in enabling me to consult the original texts. The method of transliteration used by Prof. Sayce in his Grammar is also followed in the Notes at the end of the texts.

E. A. BUDGE.

CHRIST'S COLLEGE, CAMBRIDGE,

May, 1880.

Battle-scene. Relief from Kouyunjik.

Representations of columns. Relief from Kouyunjik.

CONTENTS.

ERRATA.

Page 1, line 8, read		instead of	
" 6, " 15, "		" "	 in both places.
" 9, note *b*, "		" "	
" 9, " *d*, "		" "	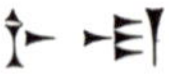
" 9, " *d*, "		" "	
" 18, line 53, "	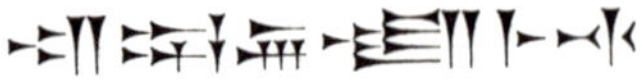	"	
" 20 " 22, "		instead of	

EXTRACT FROM THE

ARABIAN WAR OF ASSURBANIPAL.

(Smith's *History of Assurbanipal*, p. 290–294.)

A.

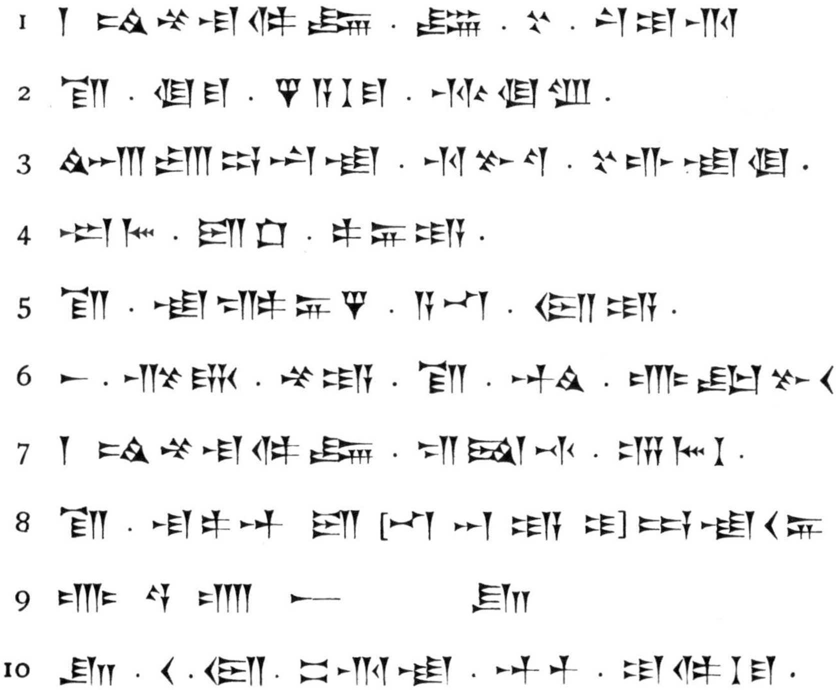

11 〔cuneiform〕

12 〔cuneiform〕

13 〔cuneiform〕

14 〔cuneiform〕

15 〔cuneiform〕

16 〔cuneiform〕

17 〔cuneiform〕

18 〔cuneiform〕

19 〔cuneiform〕

20 〔cuneiform〕

21 〔cuneiform〕

22 〔cuneiform〕

23 〔cuneiform〕

24 〔cuneiform〕

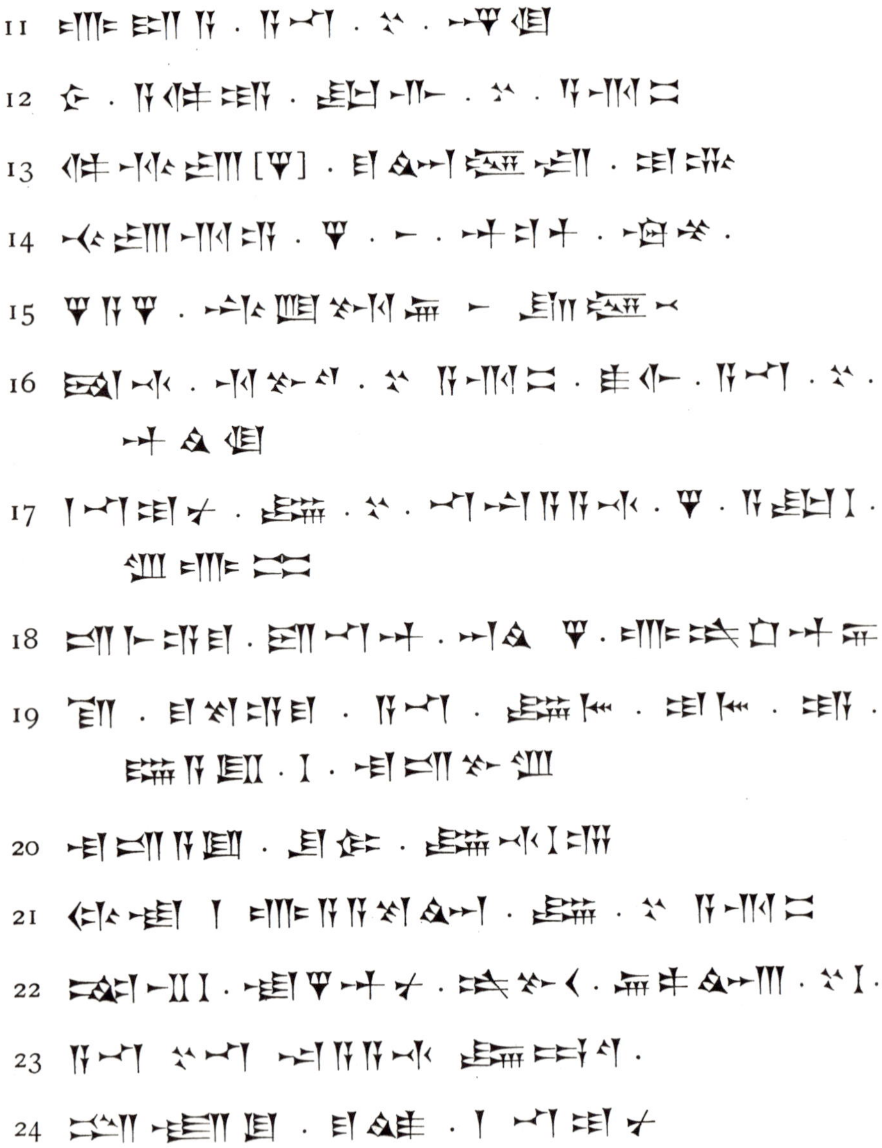

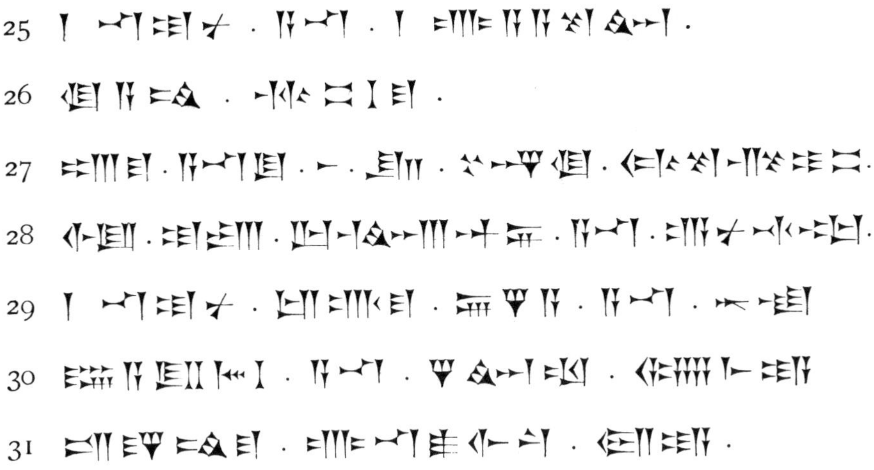

B.

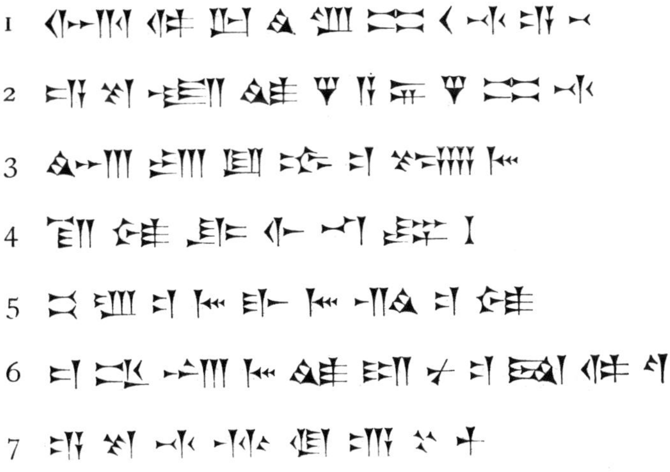

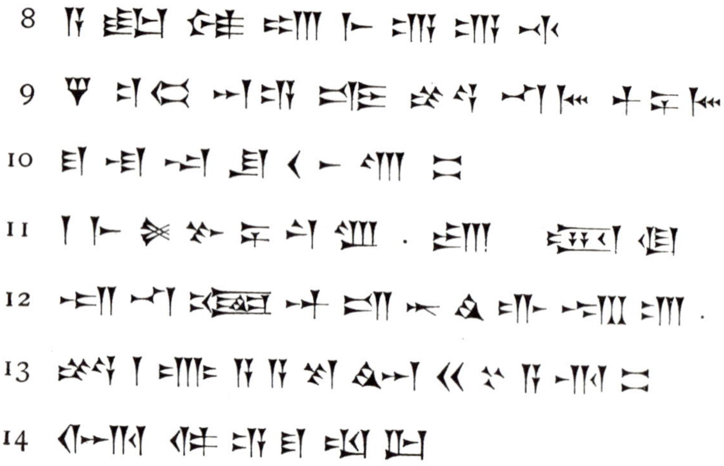

ANNALS OF SENNACHERIB

CALLED

THE TAYLOR CYLINDER.

Col. iii. 66 to Col. iv. 20.

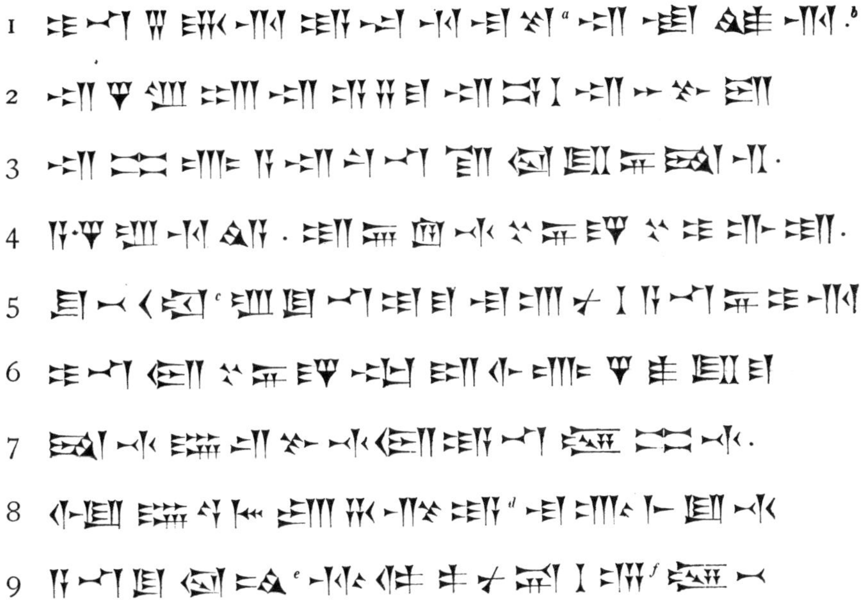

VARIANTS:

10 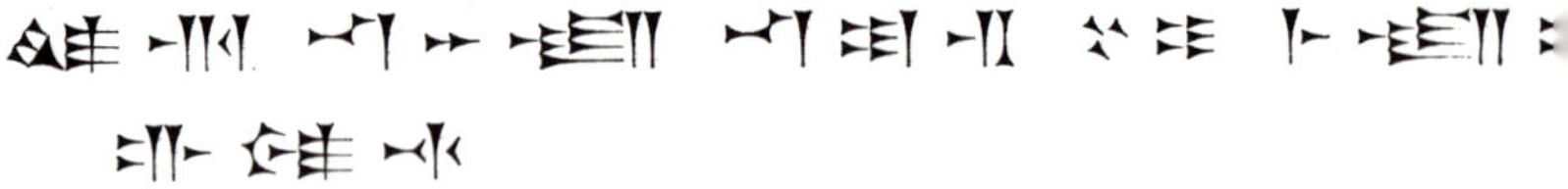

11 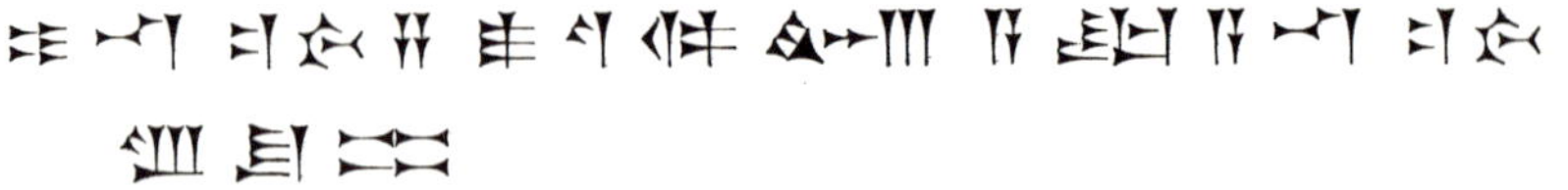

12 

13 

14 

15 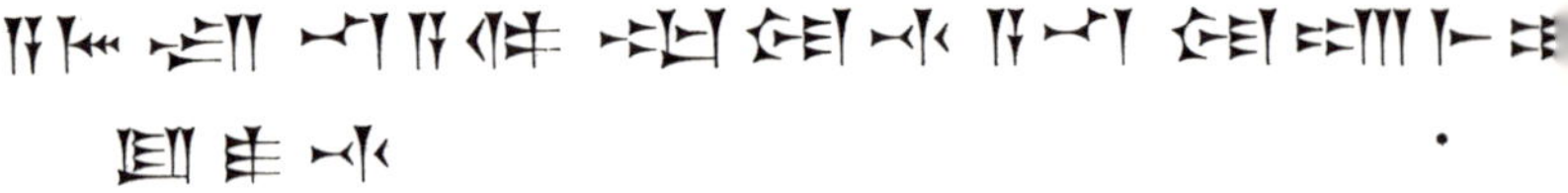

16 

17 

18 

19 

20 

VARIANT: [a] 

21 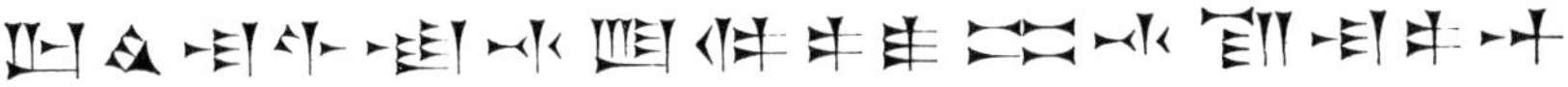

22 

23 

24 

25 

26 

27 

28 

29 

30 

31 

32 

VARIANTS: [a]  [b] 

[c]  [d] 

33 

34 

35 

36 

37 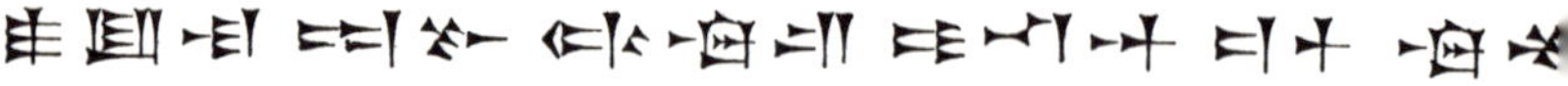

MISSION OF

GYGES, KING OF LYDIA, TO ASSURBANIPAL.

Cylinder A, Column III.,

With Variant Readings from other Texts.

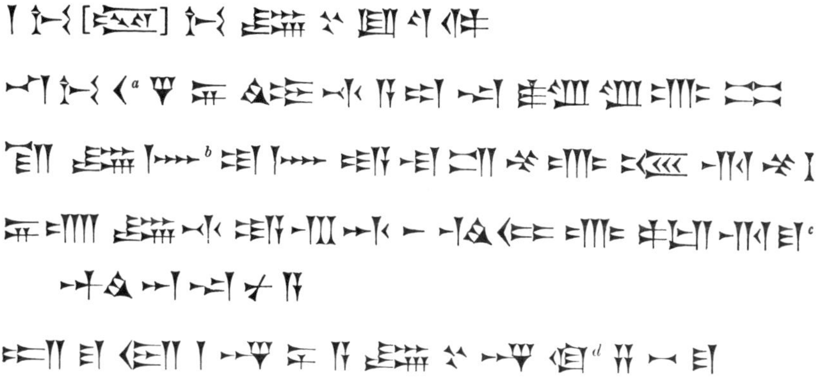

[a]  Pl. 29. 13. [b]  [c] 

[d] After  *W. A. I.* 3, pl. 29 has 
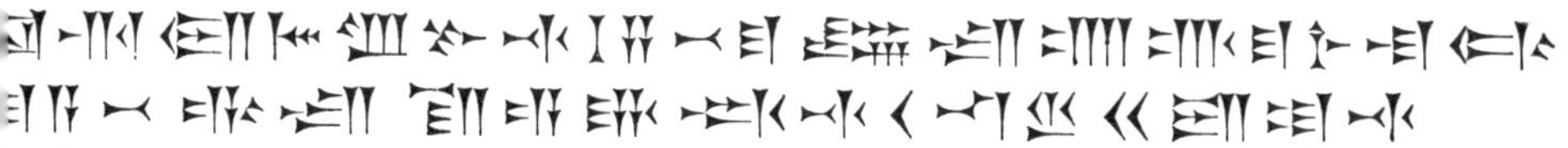
 and coincides again at line 11.

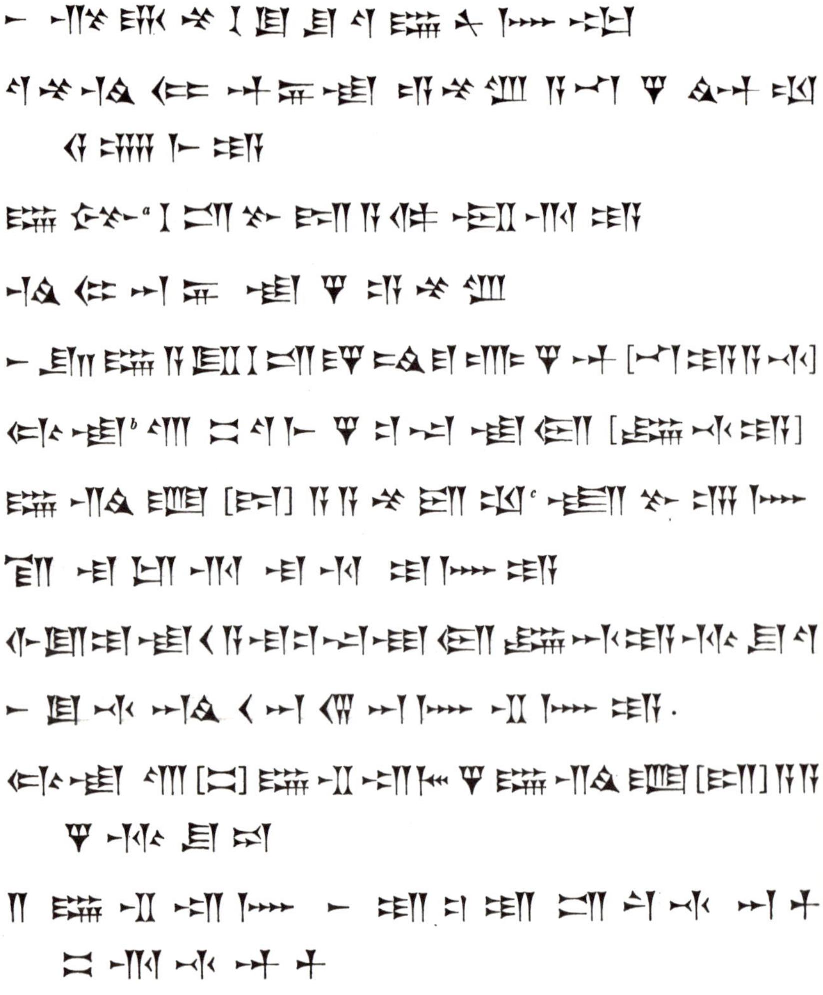

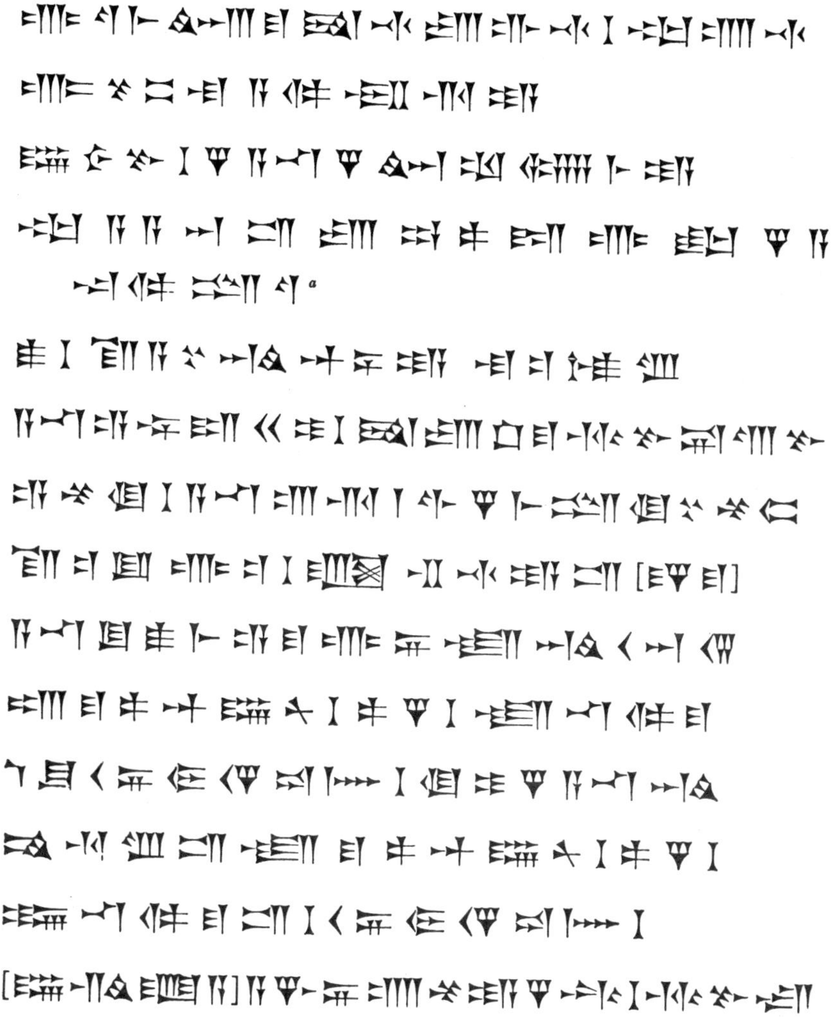

[a] 

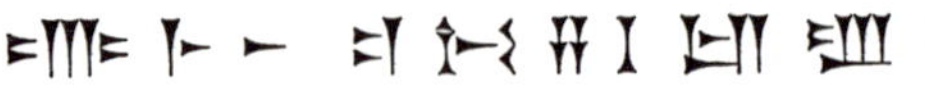

[cuneiform]

[cuneiform]
[cuneiform]

[cuneiform] [a] [cuneiform]
[cuneiform]

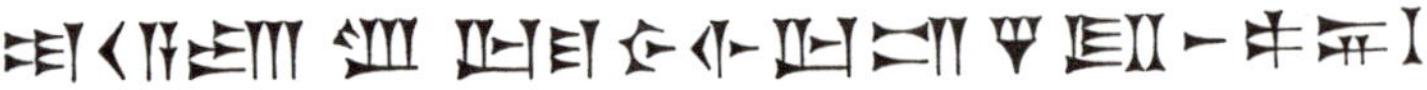

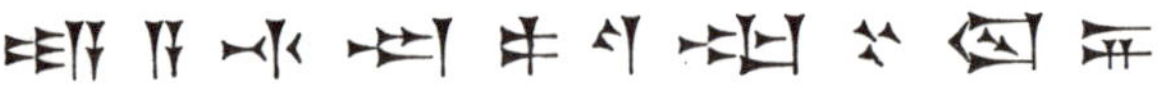

[cuneiform]

[cuneiform]

[cuneiform]
[cuneiform]

---

[a] [cuneiform].

EXTRACT FROM THE

BULL INSCRIPTION OF SENNACHERIB.

Smith, *History of Sennacherib*, p. 89–98.)

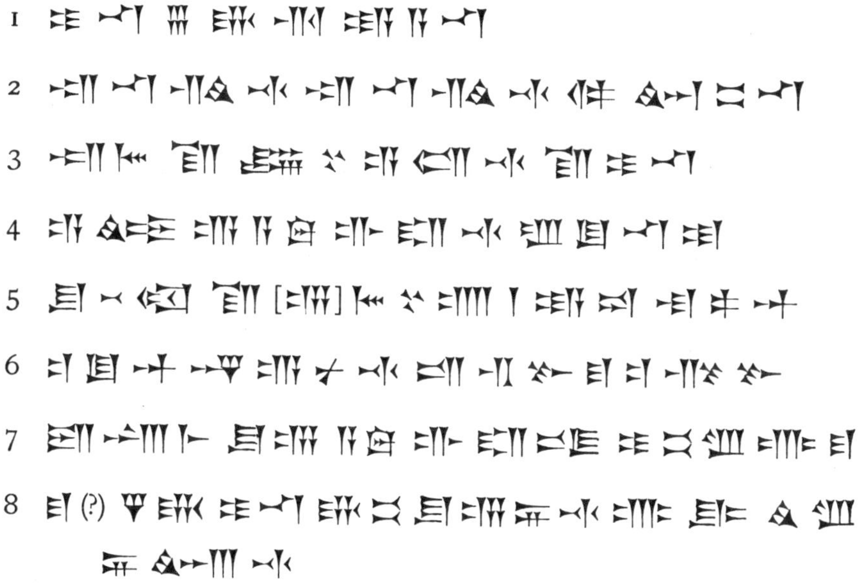

9 

10 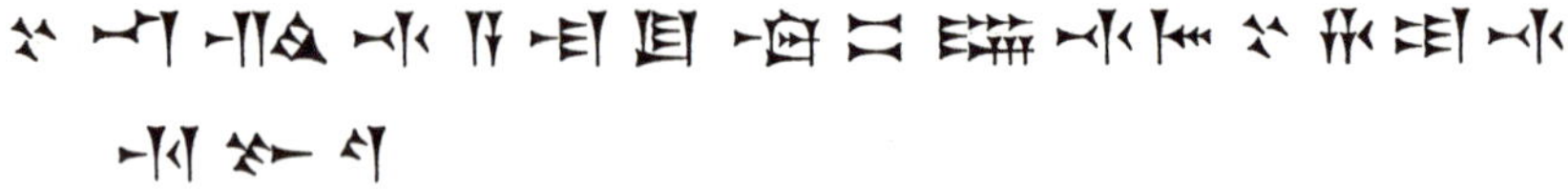

11 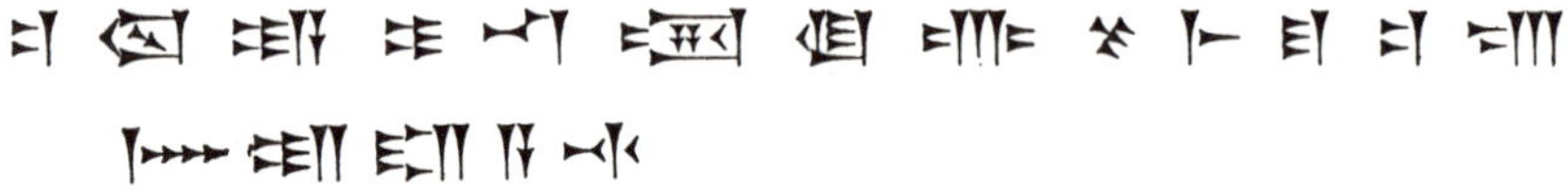

12 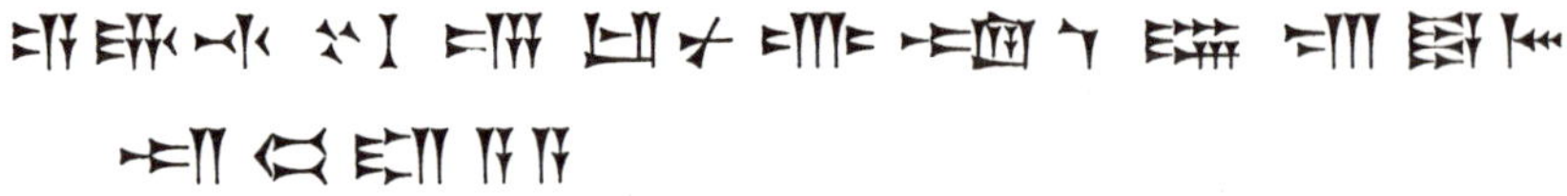

13 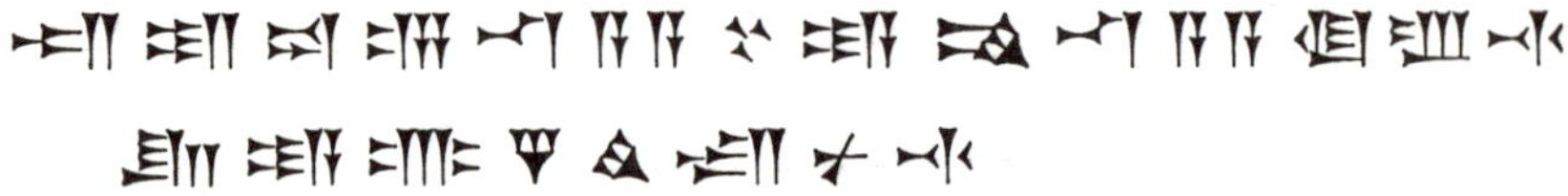

14 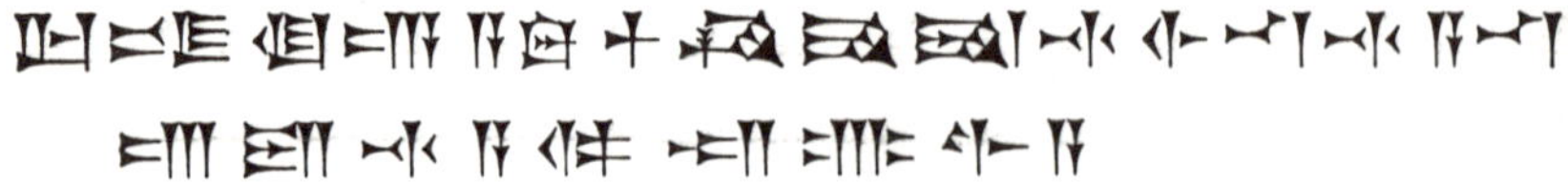

15 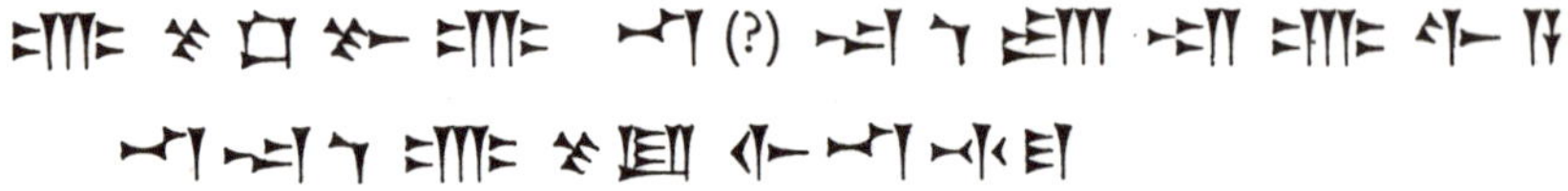

16 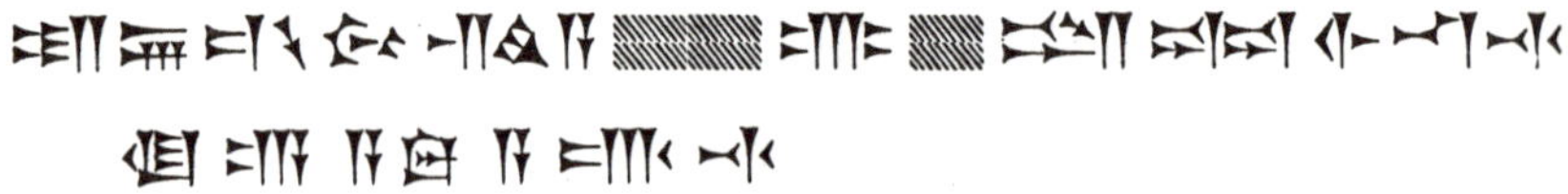

17 

18 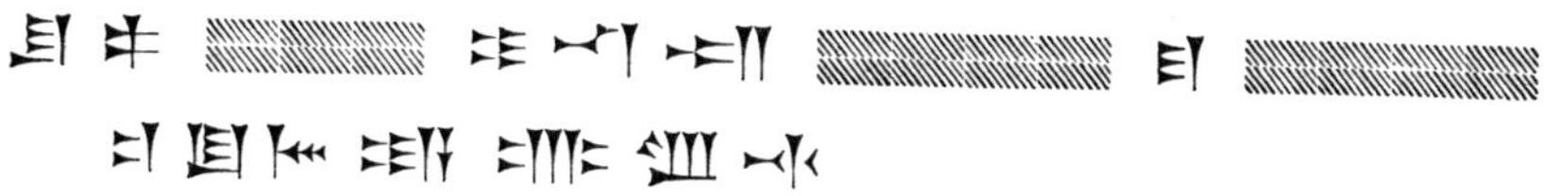

19 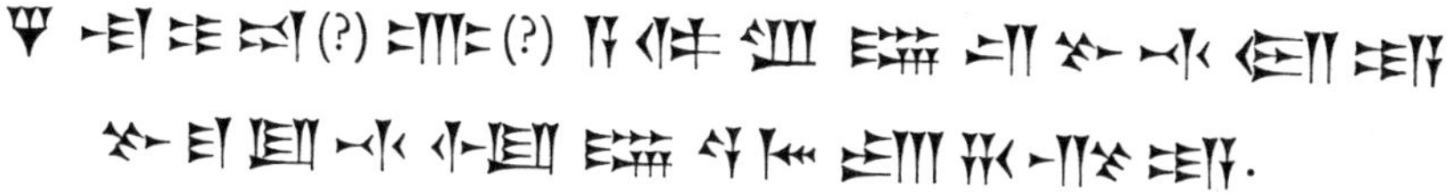

20 

21 

22 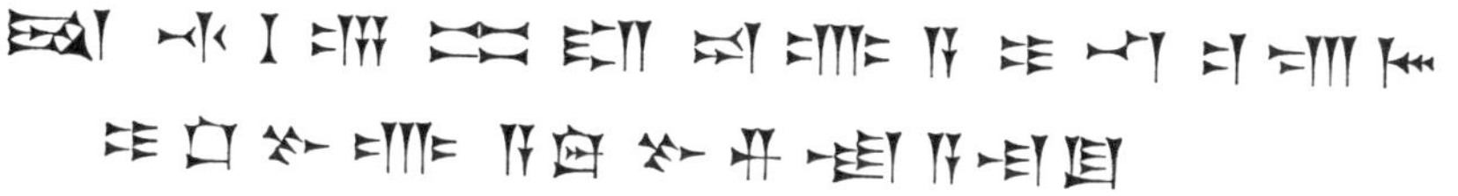

23 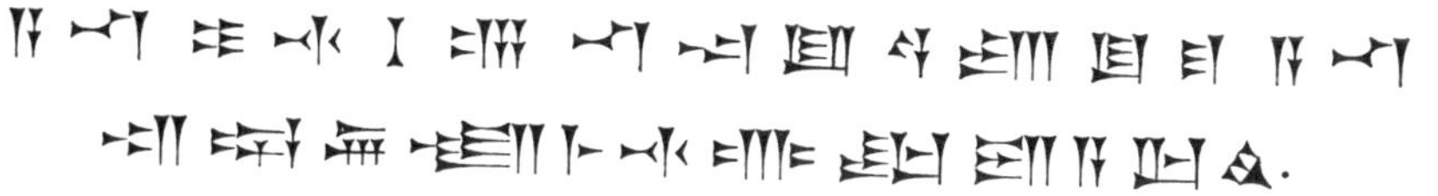

24 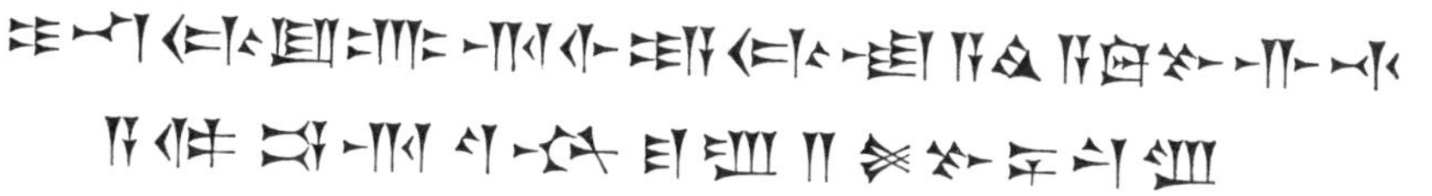

25 

26 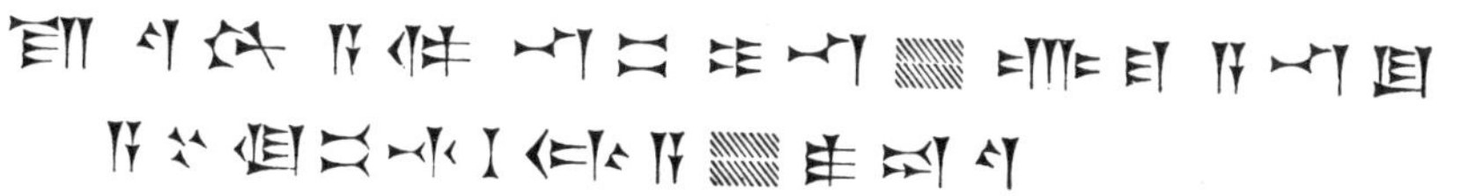

27 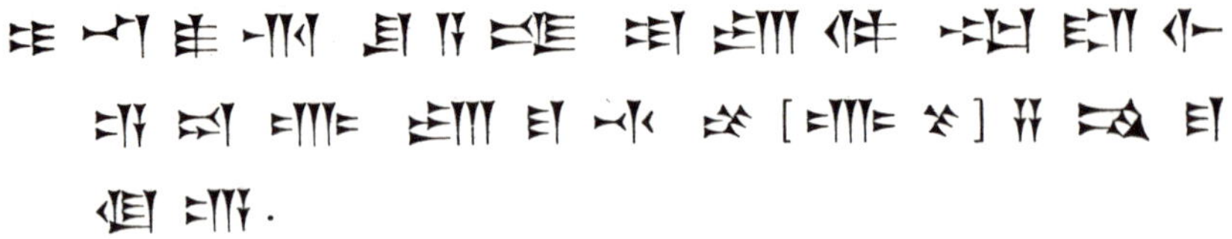

28 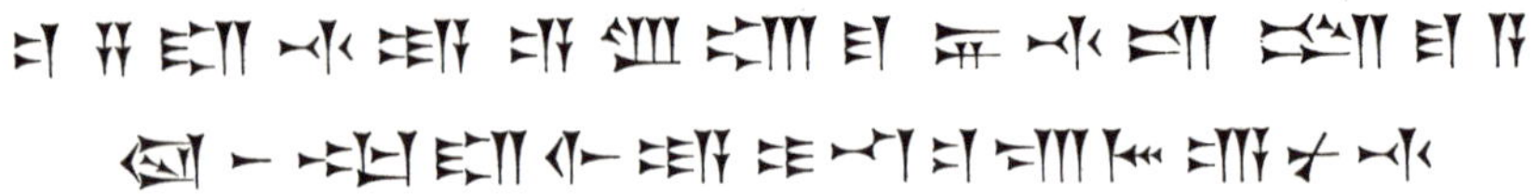

29 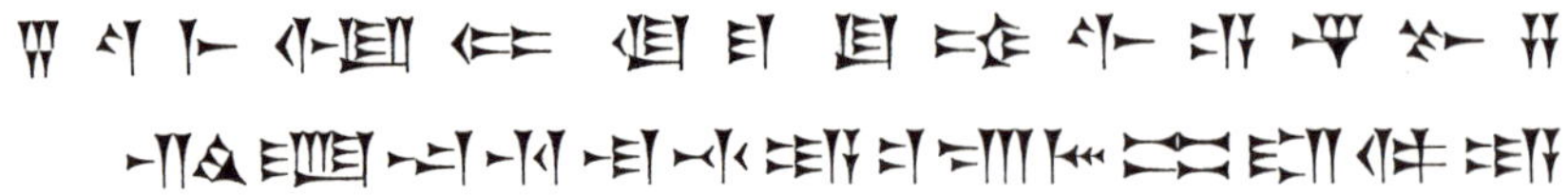

30 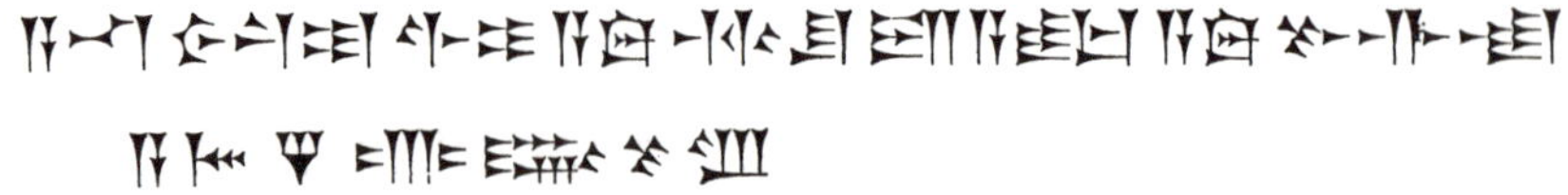

31 

32 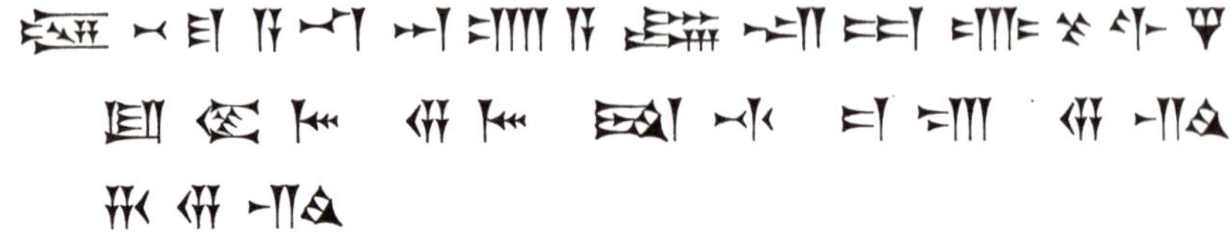

33 

34 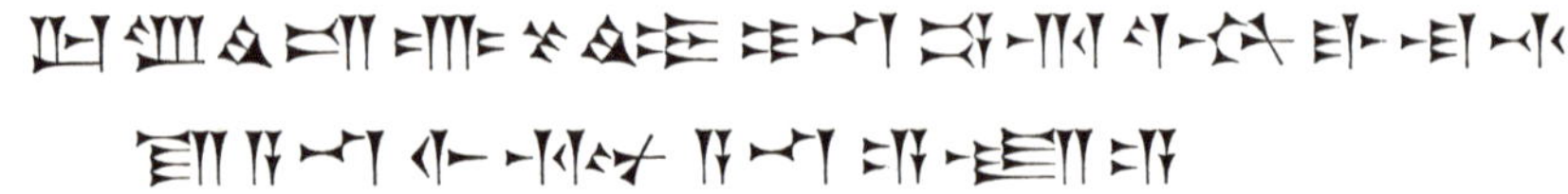

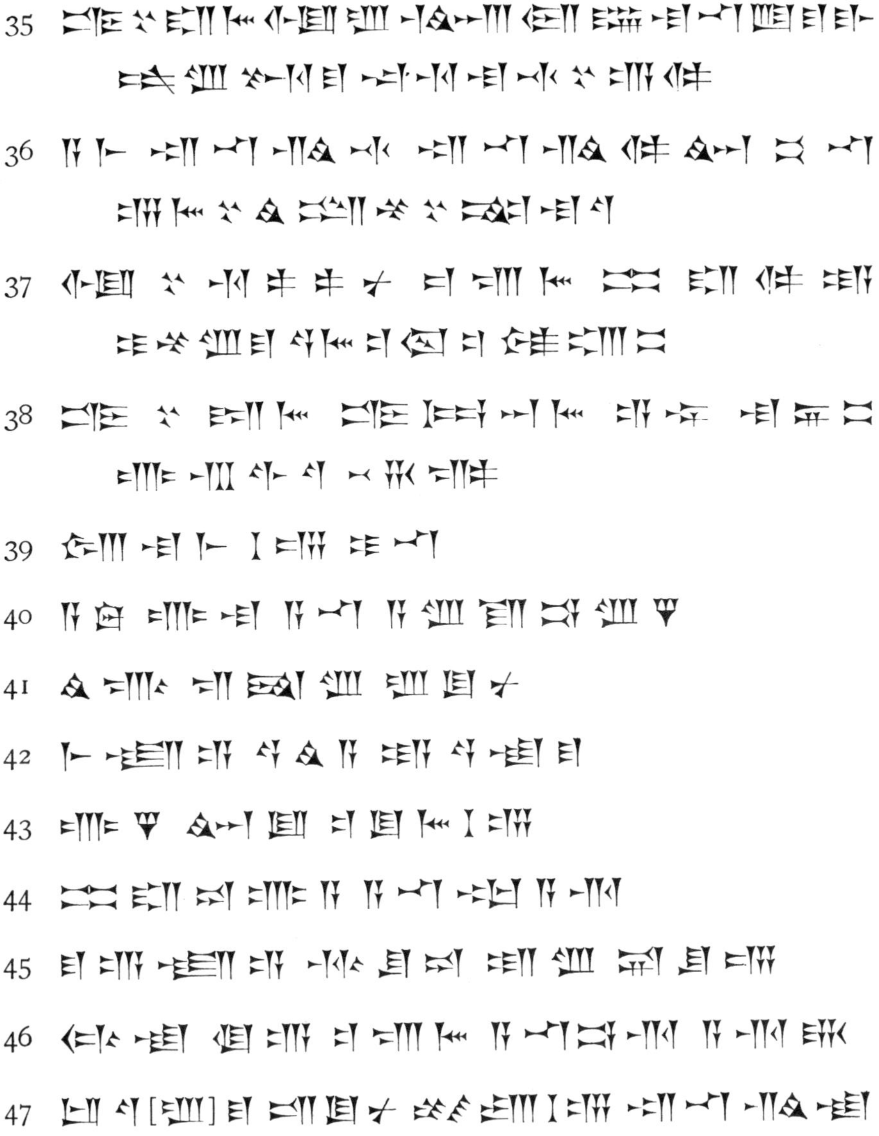
35
36
37
38
39
40
41
42
43
44
45
46
47

48 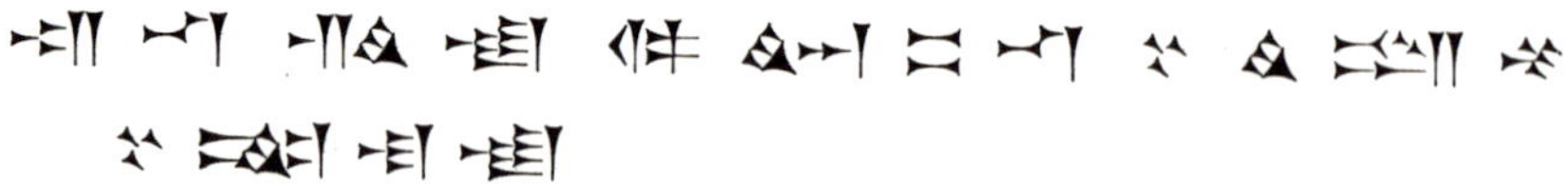

49 

50 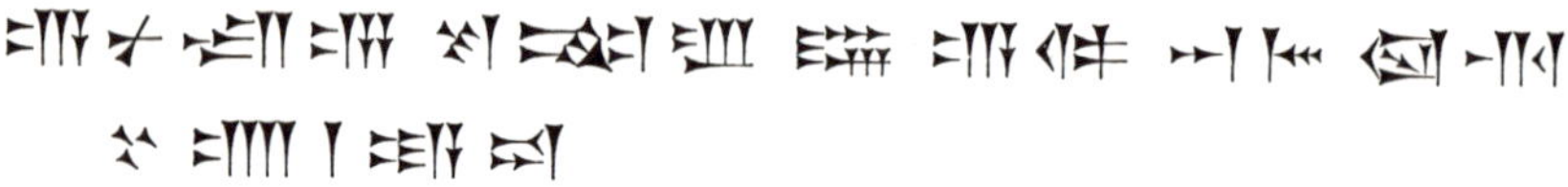

51 

52 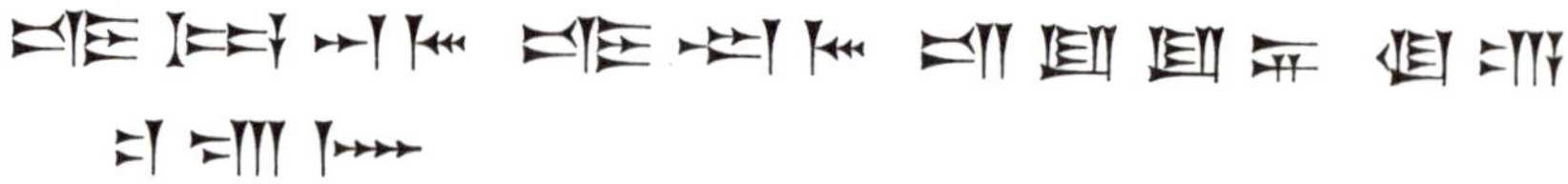

53 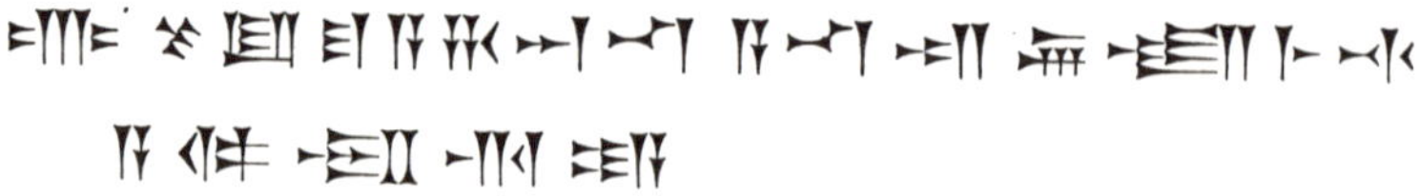

54 

55 

56 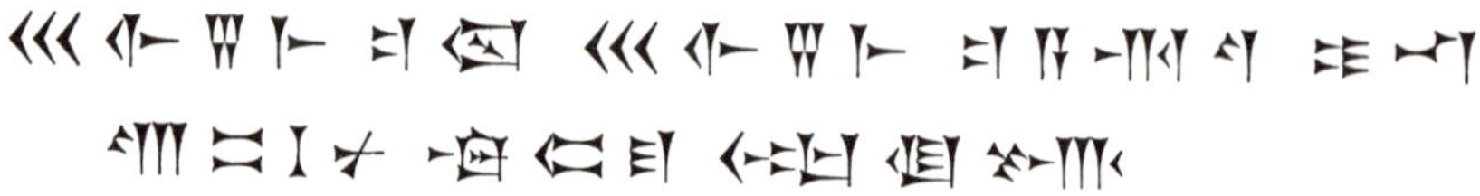

57 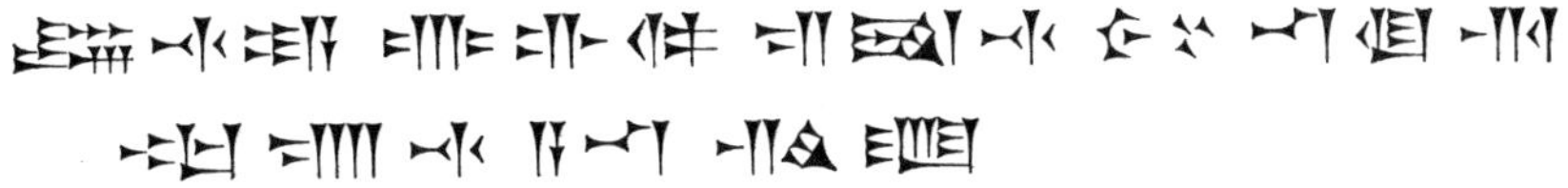

58 

59  (*W.A.I.*, I., 40, 35-42.) 

60 

61 

62 

63 

64 

65 

66 

67 

EXPEDITION OF SHALMANESER II. AGAINST HAZAEL, KING OF SYRIA.

(*W.A.I.*, 3, 5, No. 6.)

1 〔cuneiform〕
2 〔cuneiform〕
3 〔cuneiform〕
4 〔cuneiform〕
5 〔cuneiform〕
6 〔cuneiform〕
7 〔cuneiform〕
8 〔cuneiform〕
9 〔cuneiform〕
10 〔cuneiform〕
11 〔cuneiform〕
12 〔cuneiform〕
13 〔cuneiform〕
14 〔cuneiform〕
15 〔cuneiform〕
16 〔cuneiform〕
17 〔cuneiform〕
18 〔cuneiform〕
19 〔cuneiform〕
20 〔cuneiform〕
21 〔cuneiform〕
22 〔cuneiform〕
23 〔cuneiform〕
24 〔cuneiform〕
25 〔cuneiform〕
26 〔cuneiform〕

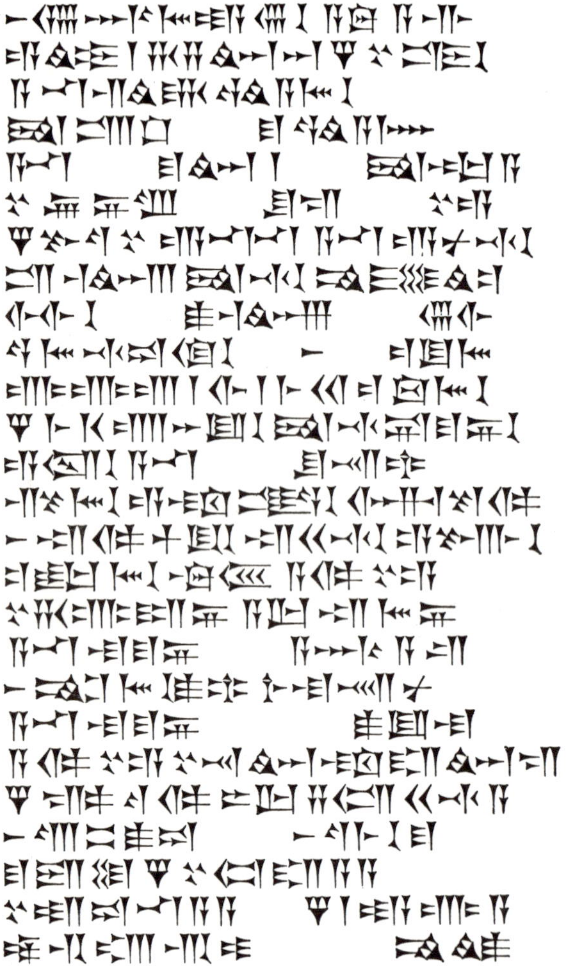

THE FIRST

EGYPTIAN WAR OF ASSURBANIPAL.

(*W. A. I.* III., pl. 28, line 1, to pl. 29, line 2.)

1 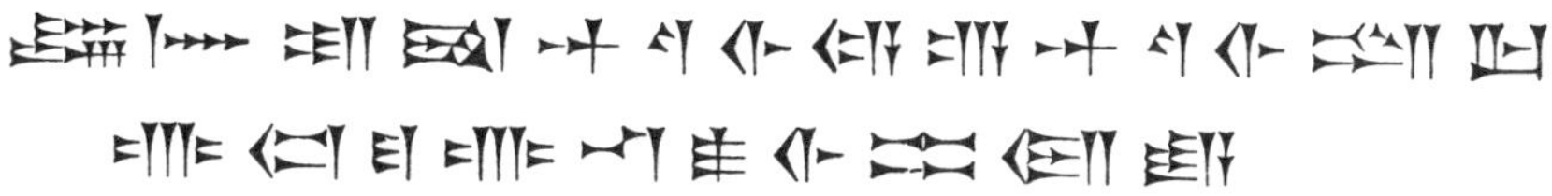

2 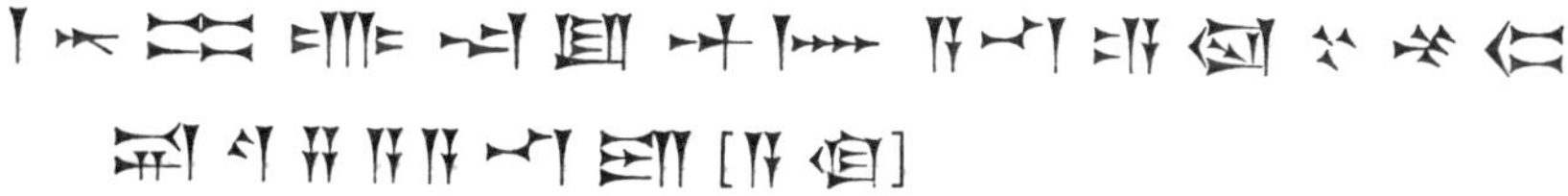

3 

4 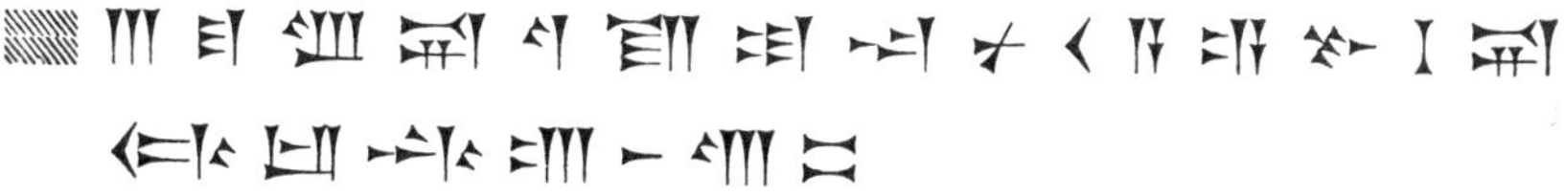

5 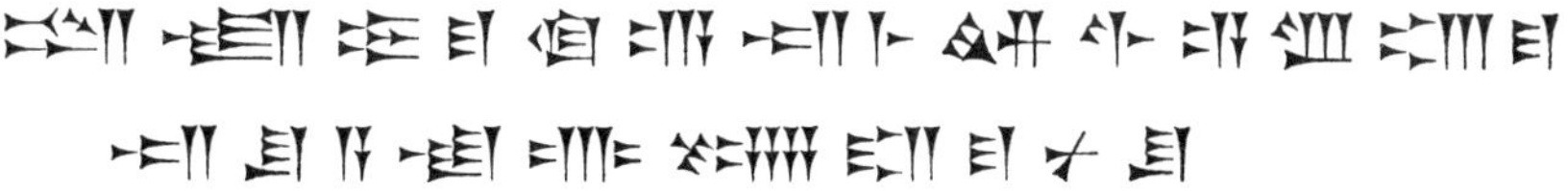

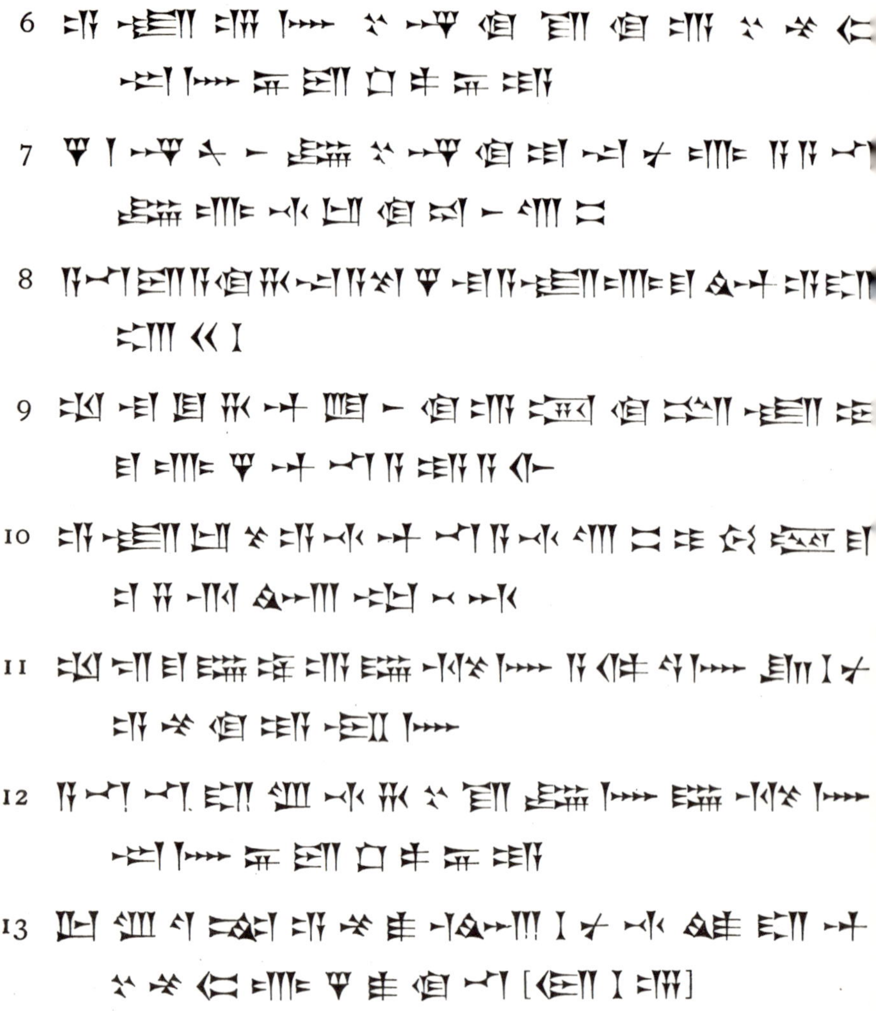

14 

15 

16 

17 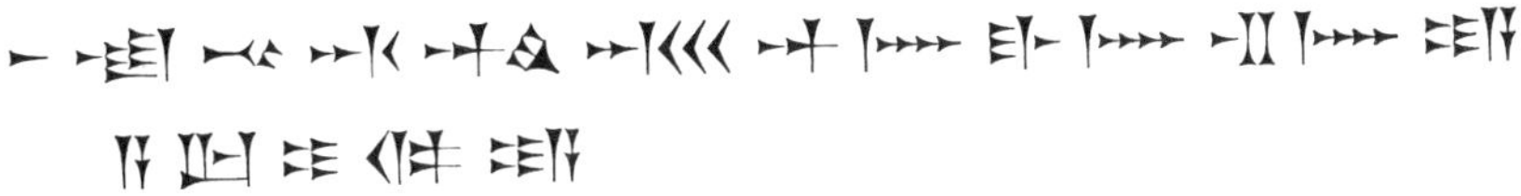

18 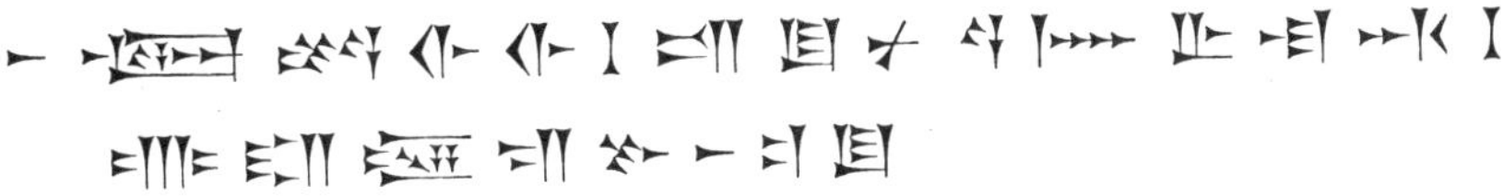

19 

20 

21 

22 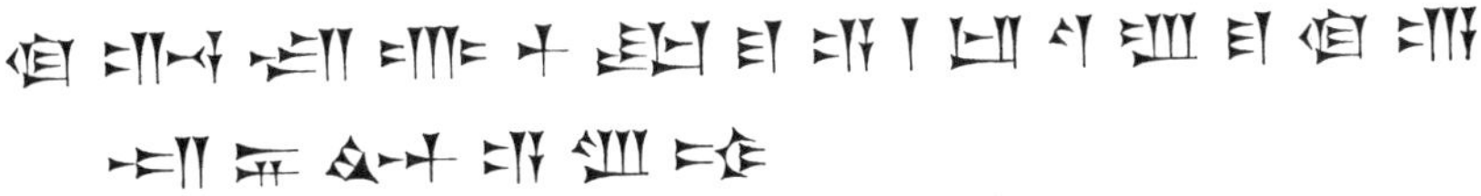

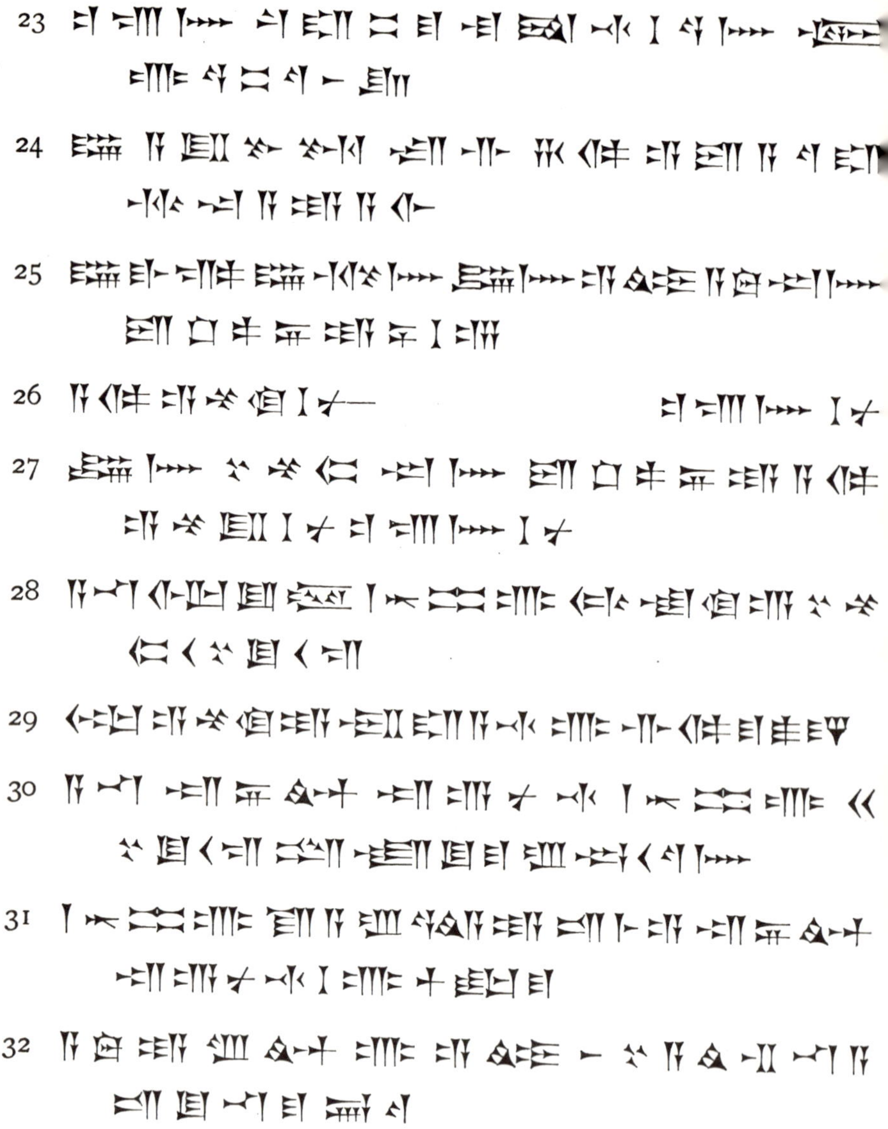
23
24
25
26
27
28
29
30
31
32

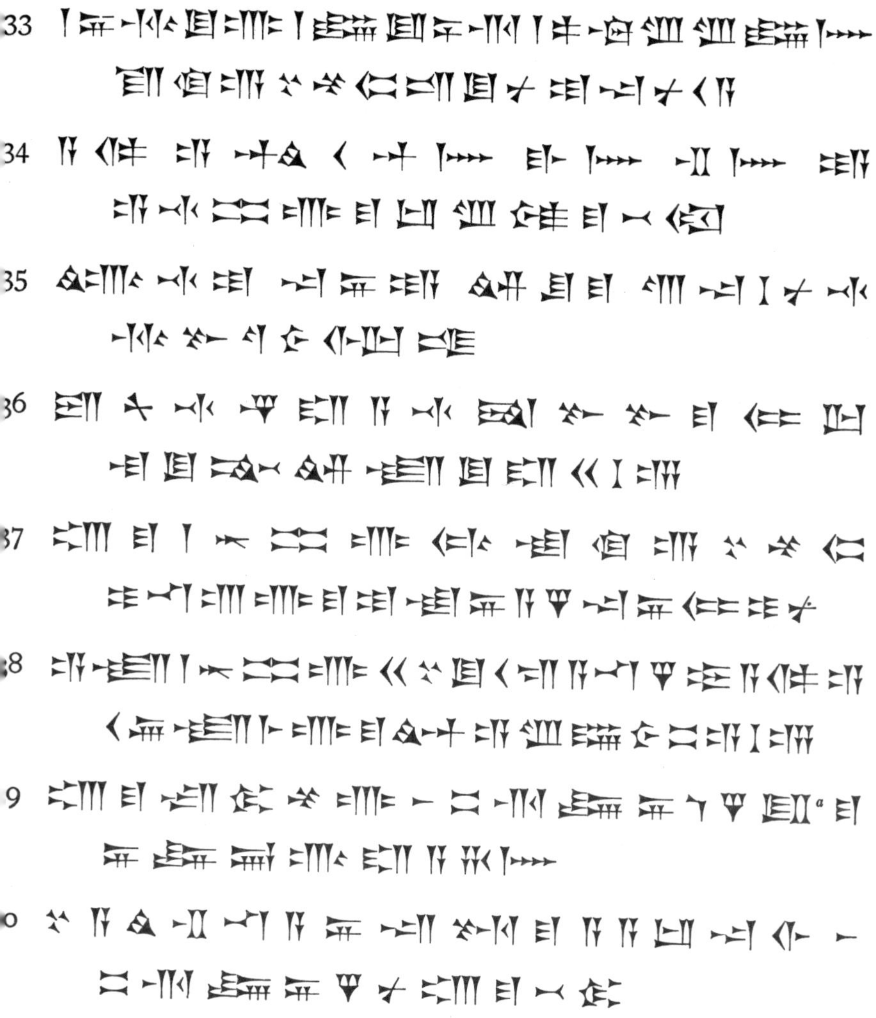

---

[a] .

41 

42 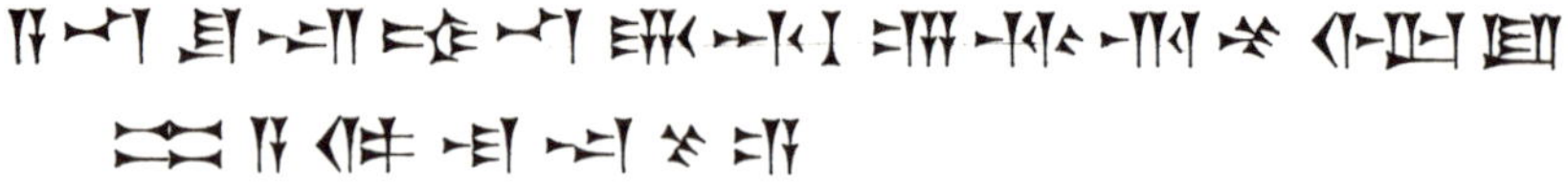

43 

44 

45 

46 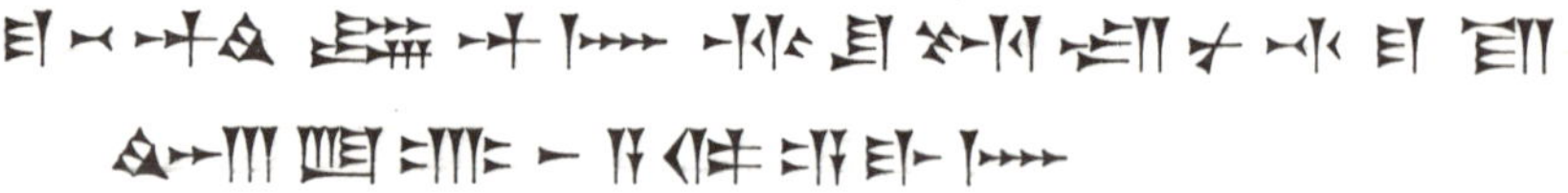

47 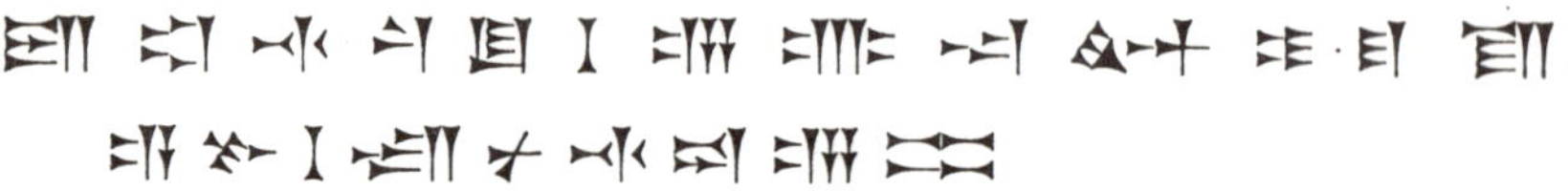

48 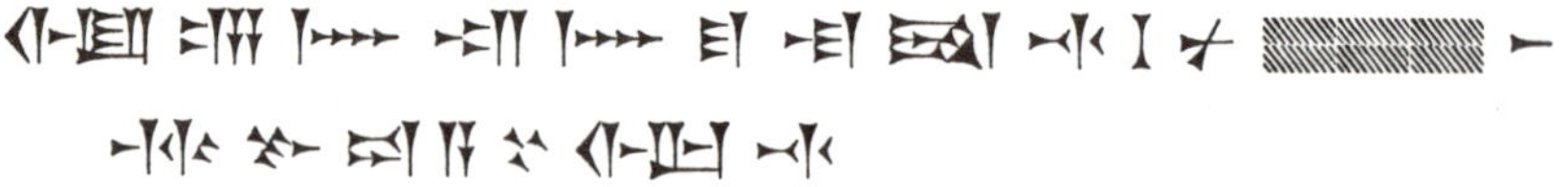

49 

50 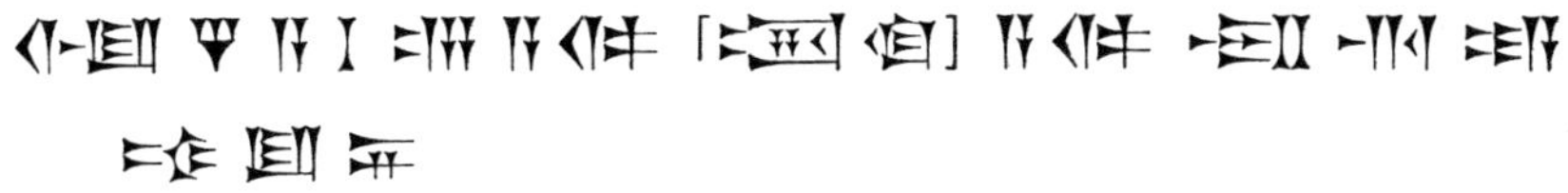

51 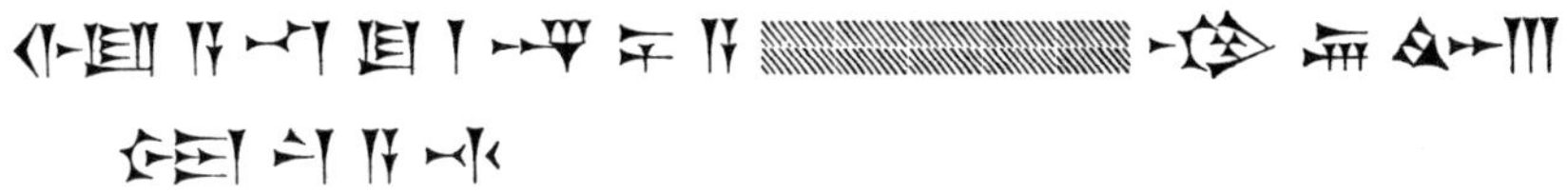

52 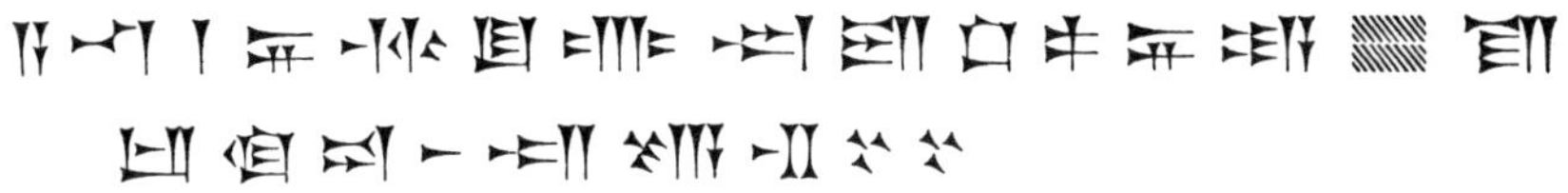

53 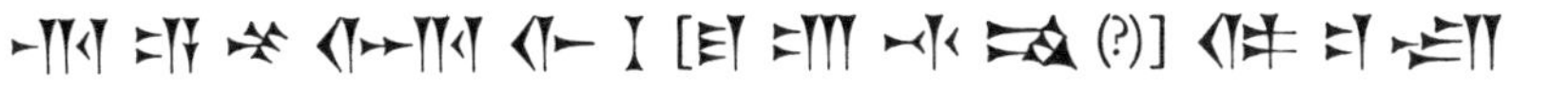

54 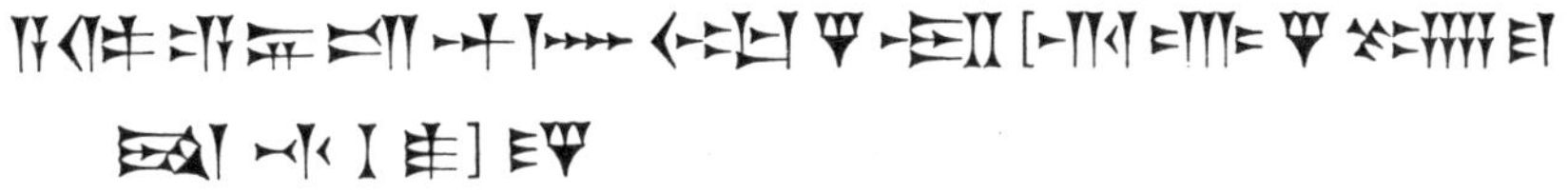

55 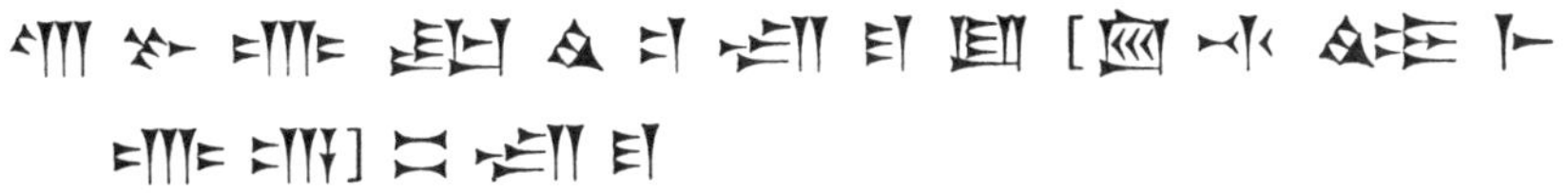

56 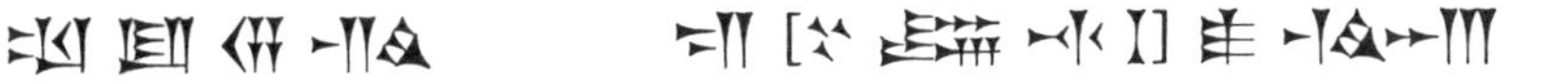

57 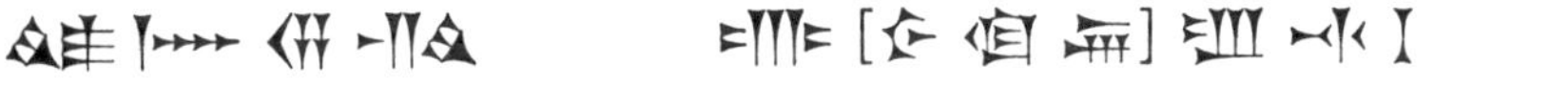

58 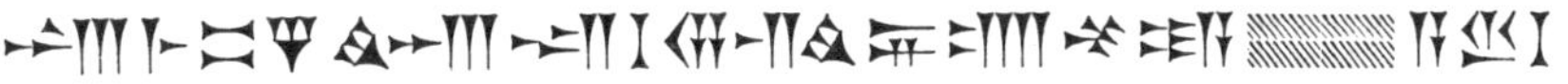

59 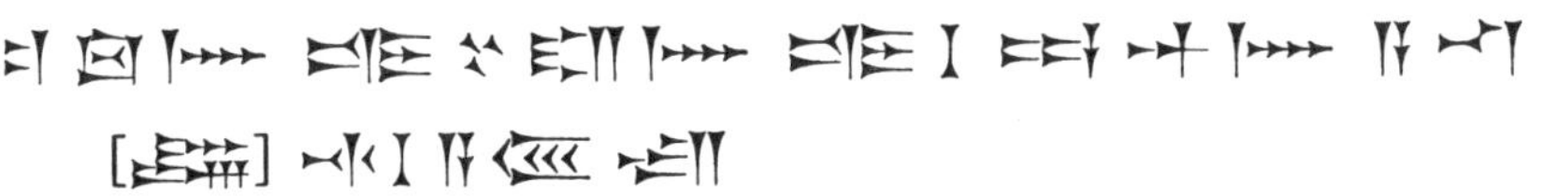

60 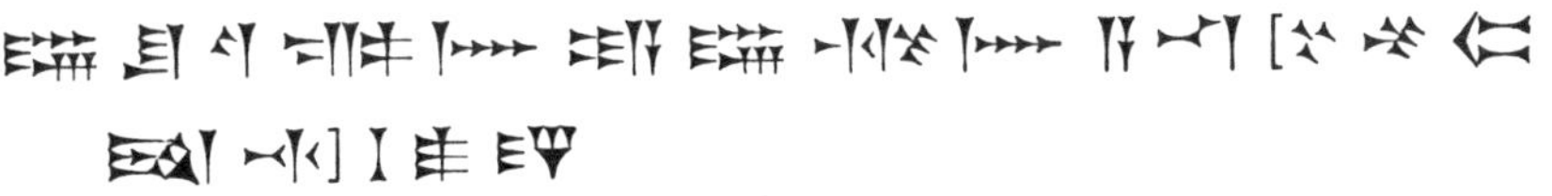

61 [illegible]

62 [illegible]

63 [illegible]

64 [illegible]

65 [illegible]

66 [illegible]

67 [illegible]

68 [illegible]

69 [illegible]

NOTES TO ARABIAN WAR OF ASSUR-BANI-PAL.

The account of this war is given by the following texts: K, 2802; K, 3096; , 562; *W.A.I.*, iii. 23, line 97, to *W.A.I.*, iii. 25, line 114; *W.A.I.*, iii. 34, line 7 to col. 8, line 57. The text given below is from K, 2802, col. 2.

The name Assur-bani-pal means "Assur creates a son."

NE

. *sar*, sub. masc. sing. cons. Heb. שַׂר.

mat or *mada*, "land," from Accadian *ma* with *da*, Accadian individualising affix. Borrowed by Arameans from Accadians under the form of מתא. See Sayce, *Assyrian Lectures*, and *W.A.I.*, ii. 39, 4.*

ka-ad-ri, the Biblical קֵדָר. The country inhabited by the descendants of Ishmael (Gen. xxv. 13, Cant. i. 5). The Rabbins call all the Arabians universally by this name (Gesenius).

. *sa*, rel. pron., identical with later Heb. שֶׁ in Canticles, Judges, and Ecclesiastes (Sayce, *Grammar*, p. 45).

cima, prep. Heb. כְּמוֹ.

sāsu-va, demons. pron. with enclitic *va*, "and."

iccuru, 3rd sing. aor. Kal. Heb. נָכַר. The aorist in *u* generally denotes a perfect or pluperfect action (Sayce, *Grammar*, Trübner, p. 55).

ikhtanabbatu, 3rd sing. masc. Iphtanaal. Heb. חָבַט.

khubūt, noun, derived from above root, "spoil."

Mar-tu-ci, the Accadian name of Syria. In *W.A.I.*, ii. 50, 57, equated with the Semitic *a-khar-ri-e*, "the land which is *behind*." Comp. Heb. אַחֲרוֹן.

ardani, subs. plu. masc. The ideograph is explained by *ar-du*, "a servant," or "tributary." Heb. רָדָה, "to subdue," hence "one subdued."

dagil, from *dagalu*, "to trust upon," depending. Part. Kal.

pani-ya, "before me."

---

* Contraction for *Cuneiform Inscriptions of Western Asia*, vols i. to iv. References are made to the *Second* Edition rof. Sayce's *Grammar*.

LINE

5. *tusacnisa*, 2nd sing. aor. Shaph., "thou hast caused to submit."
sepā, "feet." Dual.

6. *ina*, prep., "in." Comp. Heb. יֵשׁ, "in," "because."
zicir, derivative from *zacaru*, "to remember." Heb. זָכַר.
sumi-ya, "my name;" *sumi* = Heb. שֵׁם.
usarbū, 3rd sing. aor. (telic), Shaph. Heb. רָבָה.

7. *s'itti*, "remainder."
nisi, "men." Comp. Heb. אֱנָשׁ.

8. *lapān*, "from before," compound prep. Comp. Heb. לִפְנֵי.
danan, "power," "might."
innabtūni, 3rd plu. masc. pluper. Niph.

9. *utsabbit*, 1st sing. aor. Pael. Comp. Arab. ضَبَّتَ.
katā, subs. dual, "the two hands." Targum קַתָּא. Aram. ܩܬܐ, "a handle.

10. *kasritu*, "bonds." Comp. Heb. קָשַׁר, "to bind."
AN-BAR, "iron." The syllabaries translate this by *parzillu*. Chald. פַּרְזֶל
Heb. בַּרְזֶל.
addi, 1st sing. aor. Kal, "I placed him;" *addi* is for *andi*; *su*, pronoun, an
va, the enclitic, from root נדה.

11. *urā*, "I drove." Comp. Heb. יָרָה.
Assur, name of the country of Assyria, the last sign in the line is the D.A
for "land."

12. For first sign see page 48, Sayce, *Assyrian Grammar*, D.P. for "woman."
Adiya, name of Arabian queen. A variant gives *A-di-e*.
sar-rat, queen, subs. cons. fem. Comp. Heb. שָׂרָה.
Aribi, Arabia. Old Test. עֲרָב.

13. *dicta-sa*, "her host," or fighters. Comp. Heb. דוּק, "to slay."
māhas's'u, for *māhadsu*, "its multitude." Heb. מְאֹד.
ad-duc, "I slew." Comp. Heb. דוּק.

14. *zirtarie-sa*, "her tent." Heb. זָרָה, "to spread out," hence a thing sprea
out, or a tent. A variant text gives E ZIN-NA, "desert house."
GIS-BAR = *isati*, *W.A.I.*, ii. 5. Heb. אֵשׁ, "fire."
acmu or *acvu*, "I burnt." 1st sing. aor. Kal. Comp. Heb. כָּוָה, "to burn.
Concerning the use of *m* or *v* see Prof. Sayce, *Assyrian Lectures*, p. 4

15. *paldhus'sa* for *paldhut-sa*, "her life."

LINE

16. *itti*, prep. "with." Heb. אֵת.
   assi, for *ansi*, 1st sing. masc. aor. Kal. Heb. נָשָׂא.
17. *Na-ad-nu*, proper name of the king of the Nabāiti. Heb. נָתָן.
   Nabāiti, a nation or tribe descended from Ishmael, Gen. xxv. 13. Heb. נְבָיוֹת.
   a-sar. Comp. Chald. אֲתַר, "place," "region," "district."
   rūku, "distant," "remote." An interesting example of the loss of ח in a word, through the softening of the pronunciation by the Assyrians. Heb. רָחוֹק. Other examples are: *imiru*, "ass," Heb. חֲמוֹר; *pitu*, "opening," Heb. פֶּתַח; *ribituv*, "a street," Heb. רְחֹבוֹת.
18. *isme*, 3rd sing. aor. Kal. Heb. שָׁמַע.
   utaggilanni, 3rd sing. aor. Pael from *dagalu*, "to trust," "support," with suffix of 1st pers. sing.
19. *matēma*, adv. of time, "in times past." Sayce, *Gram.*, 1872.
   abi, subs. plu. masc. Heb. אָב.
   D.P. MIRU-*su*, "his messenger." Comp. Heb. מָהַר, "to hasten on."
   la, "not." Heb. לֹא.
   ispuru, 3rd sing. pluperf. Arab. *sahara*.
20. *is'ālu*, 3rd sing. pluperf. Kal. Heb. שָׁאַל.
   sulum. Comp. Heb. שָׁלוֹם, "peace," "alliance."
21. *ultu*, adverb of time past, "from of old."
   Uaiteah, written also *Ya-ah-ta-a*, and *Ya-ah-lu-u*.
22. *dhe-en*, "decree," "judgment." Heb. טַעַם.
   tusānnu, 2nd sing. masc. aor. Pael. Heb. שָׁנָה, "to repeat."
   takbu, 2nd sing. masc. aor. Kal. Ch. קְבַע.
   sapākh, "destroy," imperative sing. masc.
24. *illicu*, "he had come," 3rd sing. masc. pluperf. Kal. Heb. הָלַךְ.
   makhar, "before," "in the presence of." מחר.
26. *ciām*, "thus." Heb. כֹּה.
   ikbi, 3rd sing. aor. Kal. Chald. קְבַע.
27. *umma*, "thus."
   anacu, "I." Heb. אָנֹכִי.
   ultetsibi, for *ustetsibi*, 1st sing. masc. Istaphal, "I am afflicted." Heb. עָצַב.
28. *atta*, "thou." Heb. אַתָּה.

LINE

tascun-anni, 2nd sing. masc. aor. Kal, with suffix of 1st pers. sing. masc. Heb. שָׁכַן.

29. *iplukh*, 3rd sing. masc. aor. Kal, "he feared." Chald. פְּלַח.
irsā, 3rd sing. masc. aor. Kal, perhaps רְשָׁא, "he inclined."
siltu, "peace." Comp. Heb. שלו.

31. *yunāssika*, 3rd sing. masc. aor. Pael. Heb. נָשַׁק.

B.

1. *ardi*, 1st sing. masc. aor. Kal, "I descended." Heb. יָרַד.
urkhi. Comp. Heb. אֹרַח, "road." *W.A.I.*, ii. 52, 3, gives three synonyms for the Accadian word for "road."
KHARRANU, "a road."
daragu, "a step." Aram. דרגא.
mētiku, from "*etiku*." Heb. עָתַק.
ebil, "I took," literally "I carried." Heb. יבל

2. *eteli*, 1st sing. masc. aor. Iphteal. Heb. עָלָה.
kharsāni, subs. plu. Heb. חֹרֶשׁ.
sakuti, adj. from Accadian SAK, "a head."

3. *akhtalūp*, "I passed through." Heb. חָלַף.
D.P. KISTI, "jungles." Comp. Syr. ܩܘܣܬܐ, Castel, *Lex.*, p. 796.

4. *tsulul*, "dark-places." Comp. Arab. ظَلَّ, "to be shady."
rapsu, "vast," "great."

5. *etsi*, "trees." Heb. עֵץ.
rabi, "great." Heb. רַבָּה.
kītstsu, perhaps cognate with Heb. קוֹץ, "a thorn."

6. see Lenormant, *Étude sur quelques Syllabaires*, p. 67.

7. *etetik*, "I passed through," 1st sing. masc. aor. Iphteal. Heb. עָתַק.
cirib, "within," prep.
matbar, "wilderness," "desert." Heb. מִדְבָּר.

8. *tsumme*, "subs," "famine." Comp. Heb. צום, "to fast."
dan-danti, "very great." Of Accadian origin.

9. *itstsur*, "bird," subs. cons.

LINE

9. SAM-*e*, "heaven." Comp. Heb. שָׁמַיִם.

PAZ(?)-EDINNA, lit., "desert asses." Semitic *imiri-tseri.*

paz (?) = *imiru*, "ass." Heb. חֲמוֹר.

edinna = *tsi-e-ri.* Dr. Delitzsch compares an Arabic cognate and quotes the Heb. צחר. But according to Gesenius (*Thesaurus*, p. 1163) צחר means "white" (candidus), and goes on to say that it is used of "white asses," *i.e.*, reddish with white spots, the colour which eastern nations think very highly of when found in asses, elephants, and camels. Hence this species of ass may be meant by the composer of these annals.

BAR-KAK = *tsabī*, *W.A.I.*, ii. 6, 14. Heb. צְבִי.

dāsu, *W.A.I.*, ii. 6, 16. Heb. דִּישׁוֹן.

10. *mala*, "all." Heb. מְלֵא.

basu, "existing," partic. Kal from verb *basu*, "to be."

ina-libbi, "in the midst." Heb. לֵב.

11. I × 100 *casbu*. The *casbu* = 14 miles (Sayce).

kakkaru for *karkaru*. Comp. Heb. קַרְקַר.

TA = *istu*, "from;" a variant gives *ultu*.

NINUA, D.S., "Nineveh." Biblical נִינְוֵה.

12. ALU, "city." Comp. Heb. אֹהֶל, "a tent" or "dwelling-place."

**na-ram*, "exalted," "chosen." Niphal deriv. from *rāmu*, "to be high." Heb. רום.

D.P. "Istar," one of the great goddesses worshipped by the Assyrians, daughter of Sin, the Moon god, and wife of Bel. The Biblical עַשְׁתֹּרֶת.

khirat, synonym of *assatu*, "wife." Heb. אִשָּׁה, *W.A.I.*, ii. 36, 43.

D.P. "Bel." Biblical בֵּל. One of the chief gods of the Assyrian Pantheon. See Lenormant, *La Magie*, pp. 105, 144.

13. ZIN = *tseru*, "over," "against," but a variant reads *arcu*, "after."

* Or probably "loved," Niph. of רחם.

NOTES TO TEXT OF FIFTH CAMPAIGN OF SENNACHERIB.

These expeditions to Tumurru and Cilicia took place about B.C. 699 and 698 respectively (*Sennacherib*, p. 87). The name of Sennacherib (or Sin-akhi-irba) means "The god Sin increased brothers." He reigned B.C. 705—681.

The text is given in *W.A.I.*, i. 39, 66 to 40, line 20.

LINE

1. *girri*, subs. sing. masc., "expedition." Comp. Heb. גָּרָה, "to make war;" *ina khamsa girri-ya*, "In my 5th expedition." The masculine noun takes a feminine ordinal as in Hebrew. Comp. Heb. חֲמִשָּׁה.

bakhulate, variant for *nisi*, "men," or "inhabitants," variant *nisi*, "men."

3. *kini*, subs. masc. gen. sing. Heb. קֵן.

ID-PAK = *na-as-ru*. Heb. נֶשֶׁר, "eagle."

4. *asarid*, "chief," "king," subs. sing. cons.

itstsuri, "birds," plu. gen. of *itstsur*. Heb. צִפּוֹר.

sukti, perhaps connected with Accad. SAK, a "head," hence "heights."

SAD, *D.P.* of "mountain." Comp. Arab. *saddun*, "mons."

martsi, "difficult," or "inaccessible." Comp. Heb. מָרַץ.

5. *subat-sun*, "their dwelling," subs. fem. Comp. Heb. יָשַׁב, "to dwell."

sitcunātva, "was situated and," 3rd pers. sing. Permansive, Iphteal. Comp. Heb. שָׁכַן.

nir-i. Comp. Heb. מָנוֹר, "a yoke," from נִיר, "to plough," with suffix 1st pers. pron.

6. *carasi*, "the camp." Comp. רְכוּשׁ, "wealth," "substance," and see Sayce, *Trans. Soc. Bib. Arch.*, ii. 26.

usāscin, 1st sing. masc. aor. Shaph. Heb. שָׁכַן.

7. *D.P. kurbuti-sepā-ya*, lit., "those near my feet." Heb. קָרַב, "to be near."

8. *tsabi*, "soldiers." Heb. צָבָא, a "host."

takhazi for *tamkhatsi*. A Niphal deriv. Comp. Heb. מָחַץ, "to strike."

9. AM = *ri-i-mu*, "wild bull." Heb. רְאֵם.

ikdu, "strong," "mighty."

LINE

10. *kharri*, "deserts." Comp. Heb. חֲרֵרִים.
nakhalli, "streams." Comp. Heb. נַחַל.
nādbak, "ridge" (Smith). Heb. דָּבַק, "to cleave."
melie, "ascents." Heb. עָלָה, "to go up;" like *nadie*, "gifts; *nagie*, "districts."

11. *D.P.* GUZA. Of Accadian origin. Explained by *cūs'sʹu*, *W.A.I.*, ii. 46, 50. Comp. Heb. כִּסֵּא.
astamdīkh, this reading is proved by *W.A.I.*, iii. 12, 39, for *astandikh*. *M* usually, but not always, becomes *n* before a sibilant, dental, or guttural (Sayce, *Gram.*, 1872). "I was lying." Iphtaneal of שָׁטַח.
supsuku, "impassable," Shaph. pres. permansive of פשק. Aram. פסק.

12. *astakhkhīd*, "I travel far," pres. Iphteal of שחט.
arme, "a wild sheep or goat." Syr. ארנא.

13. *eli*, "I ascended," 1st sing. masc. aor. Kal עָלָה.
bircāi, "my knees," *birka*, dual of *bircu*. Comp. Heb. בִּרְכַּיִם; cons. בִּרְכֵּי.

14. *manakhtu*, "rest," abstract subs. Comp. Heb. מְנוּחָה.
isā, 3rd dual aor. Kal of *isu*, "to have." Comp. Heb. יֵשׁ.
TAG = *abnu*, "stone." Heb. אֶבֶן.
usib, 1st sing. masc. aor. Kal. Comp. Heb. יָשַׁב.

15. A-MES = *mie*, "waters." Comp. Heb. מַיִם.
nādi, subs. sing. gen. case. Heb. נאד, a "bottle."
catsuti, generally rendered "impure," "nauseous." *mic nādi catsuti* = "its impure waters from a bottle."
lu-asti, "then I drank," 1st sing. masc. aor. Kal. Comp. Heb. שָׁתָה.
lu must be carefully distinguished from *lu* commencing the precative.

16. SU-S'I-MES = *ubani*, "peaks." Comp. Heb. בֹּהֶן.
kharsāni, gen. plu. of *kharsu*. Comp. Heb. חֹרֶשׁ.

17. *astacan*, "I establish," 1st sing. masc. pres. Iphteal.
TAKHTA = *abicta*, "overthrow." Heb. הָפַךְ.
ACS-*ud*, "I captured," 1st sing. masc. aor. Kal. Compare Arab. *kashada*.

18. *aslula*, 1st sing. masc. aor. (of motion) Kal. Heb. שָׁלַל.
salla, "spoil," deriv. from above root.
appul, 1st sing. masc. aor. Kal. Heb. נָפַל.
akkur, 1st sing. masc. aor. Kal. Heb. נָקַר.

19. *utir*, "I turned." Heb. תור.

LINE

20. *atstsabat*, 1st sing. masc. Niph. of *tsabatu*.
21. *la-pituti*, "unopened," *la*, "not;" *pituti*, deriv. from *pitu*, "to open." Comp. Heb. פָּתַח.
 dhudhi, "marshes." Comp. Heb. טִיט.
 pāskuti, "difficult."
22. *ullanua*, adv. "in former time."
23. *māmman*, rel. pron., "any one whatever." Comp. Heb. מְאוּמָה.
26. read *git-ma-lu-ti*.
27. *neribi*, "passes," Niphal deriv. Comp. עָרַב, "to enter," and see Smith, *Sennacherib*, p. 83.
 erūvva, for *erūbva*, "I entered." 1st sing. masc. aor. Kal. Comp. Heb. עָרַב.
28. *martsis*, "(with) difficulty." Adverb from *martsu*.
29. *ummani-ya*, "my army." Comp. Heb. הָמוֹן, used in this sense in Judges iv. 7, Daniel xi. 11, 12, 13.
30. *e-mur*, 3rd sing. masc. aor. Kal of *namaru*.
 e-zib, 3rd sing. masc. aor. Kal. Comp. Heb. עָזַב, "to forsake."
31. *al-ve*, 1st sing. masc. aor. Kal. Comp. Heb. לָוָה.
32. NIN-SUM-*su*, "of every kind," or "whatever its name."
 namcur, "wealth and riches." Heb. מֶכֶר.
33. *nitsirti*, "treasures." Comp. Heb. אוֹצָרוֹת.
 E-GAL, lit. "great house." Explained *W.A.I.*, iv. 5, 31 by *e-cal*. Comp. Heb. הֵיכָל, "a palace," Isai. xxix. 7.
34. *usetsāvva*, "I caused to be brought out, and," 1st sing. masc. aor. Shap. with mimmation, and enclitic. Comp. Heb. יָצָא.
 sallatis, "as spoil," or "spoil-like," adverb, formed by affixing *is* to *sallat*.
 amnu, 1st sing. masc. aor. (Telic). Heb. מָנָה.
35. *padi*. Comp. Heb. פֵּאָה, cons. פְּאַת.
 nagi, for *nangi*, "a district," from Accadian. See *W.A.I.*, ii. 1, 147.
36. *alpi*, "oxen." Comp. Heb. אֲלָפִים.

NOTES TO TEXT RELATING THE EMBASSY OF GYGES, KING OF LYDIA.

(The Text is given in *W.A.I.*, iii. 19, 5 to 42.)

LINE

5. *gūggu*, sometimes written only *gugu*. *W.A.I.*, iii. 29, 15. Comp. the Biblical Gog.

   Lūddi. Biblical לוּד.

6. *nibirti*, Niph. deriv. from *ebiru.* Comp. Heb. עָבַר.

   A-AB-BA, "sea," ideograph for *tamti.* Heb. תְּהוֹם.

7. *ismū*, 3rd plu. masc. aor. Kal. Comp. Heb. שָׁמַע.

   zicri, or, as a variant gives more correctly, *zicir*, subs. sing. masc. cons., "renown." Comp. Heb. זָכַר.

8. BIRU-MI = *suttu*, "dream," lit., "night dream." Comp. Heb. שֵׁנָה. Sayce, *Syllabary*, No. 69.

   AN = *ilu*, "god" (*W.A.I.*, ii. 31, 27). Heb. אֵל.

   banu-a, or *banu-ya*, "my creator." Comp. Heb. בָּנָה, nom agentis.

9. *tsabat*, "take," "accept," 2nd sing. masc. imperative, Kal.

10. *D.P.* NACIRI-*ca*, "enemies," subs. plu. masc. Comp. Heb. נֵכָר, with suffix *ca*, "thy," Heb. ךָ.

11. YU-*mu*, "day," subs. sing. masc. Comp. Heb. יוֹם.

    annitu, demons. pron. See Sayce, *Gram.*, p. 60.

12. *D.P.* *racbu*, var. *rakabu* (*W.A.I.*, iii. 29, 19), "messenger," or "rider." Comp. Heb. רֶכֶב, "a horseman," 2 Kings ix. 17.

15. *sa*, "when," "in," "which."

16. *D.P.* *Gimirrai.* The גֹּמֶר of Gen. x. 2.

17. *iptallakhu*, 3rd sing. masc. pres. Iphteal. Chald. פְּלַח.

19. TUCUL-*ti*, "service."

    D.P. ES'A. The goddess Istar.

    beli, subs. plu. masc. Comp. בַּעַל, "a lord."

20. *libbi*, "among."

    D.P. BIL ALANI, lit., "lord(s) of cities."

LINE

21. A cylinder brought from Nimrud by Mr. Rassam inserts before *tsi* the *D.P.* for "wood" after *ina*, which shews the after-mentioned objects were made of wood.

22. *yutammikh*, 3rd sing. masc. aor. Pael, "he bound fast." Comp. Heb. תָּמַךְ.
tamarti, "presents."
cabitti, "numerous," "many," like Heb. כֹּבֶד, "multitude," Nah. iii. 3.

23. *yusebila*, "he caused to be brought," 3rd sing. masc. aor. Shaphel. Comp. Heb. יָבַל, "to carry as gifts," Psalm lxviii. 30.

25. *istanappara*, 3rd sing. masc. aor. Iphtaneal of שׁפר. See Sayce, *Gram.*, p. 64 "he was continually sending."

26. *assu*, "besides."
amat, subs. fem. sing. Comp. Heb. אֲמָת.
KAK = *banu*, "to create;" KAK-*a*, "my creator."
itstsuru, 3rd sing. masc. pluper. Kal. Comp. Heb. נָצַר, "to protect;" *la itstsuru*, "he had not protected."

27. *e-muk*, "power," "might." Comp. Heb. עֹמֶק.
ramani-su, "of himself," reflex. pron. Its true meaning was first pointed out by Dr. Oppert (see Sayce, *Gram.*, Trübner, p. 48).

27. *icbūs*, 3rd sing. masc. aor. Kal, "he trod down." Heb. כָּבַשׁ.

28. *Pisamīlci*, a variant gives *Tusamīlci*. *Tu* as an ideograph is read *eribu*, and means "to descend," hence "a descendant of the king."
Mutsur. The Biblical מָצוֹר, "Egypt."

29. *izlū*, 3rd sing. masc. pluper. Kal, "he had thrown off." Comp. Heb. זול "to remove."
SUTUL = *niru*, "yoke." Heb. מָנוֹר from ניר, "to plough."

30. *utsalli*, "I prayed," 1st sing. masc. aor. Pael. Comp. Chald. צְלָא.

31. *pagar*, "corpse." Comp. Heb. פֶּגֶר.

32. NER-PAD-DU, rendered "attendants" (Smith).

35. *sapal*, "below." Comp. Heb. שָׁפֵל.
icbus'u for *icbusu*, "he had trodden," 3rd sing. masc. pluper. Kal. כָּבַשׁ, "to tread upon."
idpunu, 3rd sing. masc. pluper. Kal, "he destroyed." Comp. Heb. דָּפָה, "to slay."

LINE

36. *išpunu*, "he had swept," 3rd sing. masc. pluper. Kal. But Comp. Heb. סָפָה.
arcu, "afterwards."
TUR = *ablu*, "son," "after him his son."

38. *ticli-ya*, "my ministers," same root as *tucultu*.
usapriku, 3rd sing. masc. pluper. Shap. Comp. Heb. פָּרַק, "to break."
LIMITTU, "evil," "wickedness."
issacin, 3rd sing. masc. aor. Niph. Heb. שָׁכַן.
ina-pani-su, "in his time," "before him."

42. *khattu-ca*. Comp. Heb. חֵת, *abdu khat-tu-ca*, "thy reverent servant."

EXPLANATION OF IDEOGRAPHS OCCURRING IN THE BULL INSCRIPTIONS.

4. HID = *nāhru*, "river." *W.A.I.*, ii. 50, 5. Heb. נָהָר.

11. *D.P.* BAM = *mit-pa-nu*, K 2652, line 8, "bow," it is a synonym of *ka-as-tu* (*W.A.I.*, ii. 19, 7, 8). Comp. Heb. קֶשֶׁת.
D.P. MĀ-MES = *slippi*, "ships;" *e-lap-pu* (*W.A.I.*, ii. 2, 280). Aram. אִלְפָּא.
NINUA. D.S., "Nineveh." Biblical נִינְוֵה, "the fish city." To line 11, *W.A.I.*, i. 43, 24, adds *ina D.P. elippi mat Khat-ti sa ina Ninua D.S. va Tul-Barsip ebusu tamtiv luebir*. "In ships of the Hittites which I had made in Nineveh and Tel-Barsip, I then crossed the sea."

12. *D.P.* MA-LUKH, "ship" + "ruler," or "sailor." See Sayce, *Syl.*, No. 307.
Tsurrai, "Tyrians." Biblical צוֹר.

13. *Tsidūnai*, "Zidonians." Biblical צִידוֹן.
Yāvnai, "Cyprians." Comp. Biblical יָוָן.

14. *D.P.* MAS-TIGGAR, the Tigris river.

22. *D.P. purattu*, the river Euphrates. Biblical פְּרָת. In Accad. *pur-rat*, "the winding river."

24. *casbu*, a ground measure of about 14 miles (Sayce, *Records of the Past*, vol. i. p. 166). It became later a measure of time equal to 2 hours.

29. MI = *musu*, "night," *W.A.I.*, ii. 1, 149. Heb. אֶמֶשׁ.
eribu, *W.A.I.*, ii. 39, 15. Heb. עֶרֶב.

LINE

31. TIG = *cisadu*, "bank," see Sayce, *Syl.*, No. 161, a variant gives *cisadi* (the bank of) which proves the reading. Lenormant compares Ghez, *chĕsădĕ*.

32. *D.P.* E.A. For an account of the part played by this god in the Assyrian mythology, see Lenormant, *La Magie*, pp. 145.

D.P. NIKI, "victims," plu. of *niku*, "offering," "sacrifice." Comp. Heb. נְקָה.

CU-MES = *ellu*, "high," "noble," "precious."

KHA = *nunu*, "fish." Heb. נוּן.

35. *D.P.* CURRA = *s'us'u*, "horse," lit., "the animal from the east." Heb. סוּס.

38. *D.P.* S'ULSA = *parratu*. Heb. פֶּרֶא. Comp. Heb. פָּרָה, "cow." Sayce, *Syl.*, No. 515.

40. *D.P.* *Ulai*. Comp. Biblical אוּלַי.

55. RAPAS-*tiv*, "great," "vast," see *Syl.*, No. 146.

56. SI = *alapu*, "a thousand." Heb. אֶלֶף, *Syl.*, No. 331.

ME = *meh*, "a hundred." Heb. מֵאָה, *Syl.*, No. 434.

58. CI-MAS'. The syllabaries translate MAS' by *tsabu*, "a soldier," and CI is the *D.A.* for "place." Hence the whole ideograph means the "place of soldier(s)," or "camp," and is to be read *carasi*.

EN-NAM, "lord" + "prefect." *Nam* is explained by *pikhatu* (Heb. פַּחַת, *W.A.I.*, iv. 69, 59.

NOTES TO PAGE 20.

1. SU = *essutu*, "time," "for the 16th time," for *edsutu*. Cognate to Heb. חדיש.

D.P. *Purrat*. Euphrates.

2. *ebir*, 1st sing. masc. aor. Kal. Heb. עָבַר.

D.P. *Khat-tu*. "The Hittites."

7. *būt*, "the entrance of," subs. sing. cons., lit., "the coming." Heb. בּוֹא.

Libnana. Biblical לְבָנוֹן.

12. *bit-khallu*, generally translated "carriages," or "battering rams."

13. ZI = *napistu*, "soul," "life." Sayce, *Syl.*, No. 80. Comp. Heb. נֶפֶשׁ.

15. *D.P.* *Dimaski*, "Damascus." דַּמֶּשֶׂק.

etsir, 1st sing. masc. aor. Kal. Comp. Heb. עָצַר.

LINE

D.P. KHIR = *ciru*, "an enclosure (of trees)." Sayce, *Syl.* 276.

accis, "I cut down," see *Grammar*, p. 92. Heb. נָכַס.

19. NE = *isatu*, "fire." Heb. אֵשׁ.

ASR-*up*, 1st sing. masc. aor. Kal. Comp. Heb. שָׂרַף.

22. SAK = *risu*, "head." Heb. רֹאשׁ.

tsalam, "an image," subs. sing. cons. Comp. Heb. צֶלֶם.

24. *madatu*, for *mandattu*, "tribute," "something given." Comp. Heb. נָתַן, "to give." Chald. מַתְּנָן, "gifts." Dan. ii. 6.

25. YAHUA, "Jehu." יֵהוּא, king of Israel.

khūmri, "Omri." עָמְרִי. This should be "Jehu of the *house* of Omri."

amkhar, "I received." Heb. מָחַר.

NOTES TO TEXT OF FIRST EGYPTIAN WAR OF ASSUR-BANI-PAL.

1. *tsi-it*, "rising," lit., "the going forth." Heb. יָצָא.

D.P. SAM-SI, "the sun-god." Heb. שֶׁמֶשׁ.

e-rib, "the going down." Heb. עֶרֶב.

illicunivva, 3rd plu. masc. pluper. Kal, "they had come and." Heb. הָלַךְ, with mimmation and enclitic *va*.

2. *Tarkū*. Biblical תִּרְהָקָה.

balu, "without." Comp. Heb. בְּלִי.

ecim, "capture," subs. sing. cons.

yustamtsā, 3rd sing. masc. aor. Iphtael, "he hastened." Heb. שָׁמַץ.

ippalcit, 3rd sing. masc. aor. Niphalel, with *ul*, "not," "it passed not away." See *Assyrian Lectures*, p. 113.

emīs, "he despised," 3rd sing. masc. aor. Kal. Heb. מָאַס.

5. *D.P. Meimpi.* Biblical מֹף; Greek Μέμφις.

7. *D.P. Assur-akha-iddina*, "Assur gave a brother," Esarhaddon. Biblical אֵסַר־חַדּוֹן.

ipkidu, "he had appointed," 3rd sing. masc. pluper. Kal. Heb. פָּקַד.

8. *yumāhera*, "he hastened forth." Heb. מָהַר.

10. *ipsēti*, subs. fem. plu., "deeds, actions," from *episu*.

LINE

annāti, demons. pron. fem.

itsarīkh, "it was stricken down,"* 3rd sing. masc. aor. Niph.

11. *D.P.* TUR-DAN, the "tartan." Of Accadian origin. The Biblical תַּרְתָּן of Isa. xx. 1.

MAKH = *rūbu*, "great." *W.A.I.*, ii. 31, 18. Heb. רָבַב.

13. *usāscina*, 1st sing. masc. aor. Shaph.

16. URU = *kablu*, "battle." Cf. Heb. קָבַל, "to be opposed to."

ME = *takhatsu*, "fight," for *tamkhatsu*. Sayce, *Syl.*, No. 88.

15. *Cūsi.* Comp. Heb. כוש. But for a learned dissertation on Egypt and Cush see Lenormant's paper in *Trans. Soc. Bib. Arch.*, vol. vi. part 2.

16. *is'dira*, 3rd sing. masc. aor. Kal, "he set in array." Chald. סָדַר.

mekhrit, "in front of."

17. 30 = "the Moon-god." God of the month, or 30 days.

18. SI-SI = *abicta*, "overthrow." Heb. הָפַךְ.

yuras's'ibu, 3rd plu. masc. pluper. Pael, "they ran through." Arab. *rasaba*.

21. *ana-suzub*, "for the saving of." Shaphel pass. infin. Heb. עָזַב.

napisti, subs. sing. gen. case. Heb. נֶפֶשׁ.

ircab, "he sailed," literally "he rode." Heb. רָכַב.

22. *yuvas's'ar*, or *yumassar*, "he abandoned," 3rd sing. masc. aor. Pael. Heb. מָסַר.

e-dis, "alone," "singly." Comp. Heb. אֶחָד.

ipparsid, "he fled away." And see Sayce, *Gram.*, Trübner, p. 97.

D.P. Niah. Biblical נא of Ezek. xxx. 14, or Thebes.

25. *D.P.* RAB-SAK, "chief of the princes," the "Rabshakeh" (רַבְשָׁקֵה, 2 Kings xviii. 17.

KAK-*sūn*, "the whole of them;" KAK = *calu*, "all." Comp. Heb. כֹּל.

28. *khullūk*, "dispersion," "driving out." Comp. Heb. חָלַק.

30. *malac*, "journey." Comp. Heb. מַהֲלָךְ.

100 = *arkhu*, "a month" (Sayce, *Syl.*, No. 109). Heb. יֶרַח.

32. *D.P. Yaruah*, the Nile. This is the יְאֹרָה of Exod. i. 32. The form *yauri va matati-sunu* (their rivers and countries) occurs *W.A.I.*, iv. 44, 21.

akhi-ennā, or *akhi-anna*, "this side;" *akhi* = Heb. אח; *anna*, demons. pron.

madaktu, "a fortress." Heb. דכא, דקק.

33. *Nicu*, "Necho." Heb. נְכוֹ.

* Or, "it cried out."

LINE

34. *adē*, "the oaths." Schrader, הודה ; Norris, ידע ; Sayce, עֵד.
etikū, "they transgressed," 3rd plu. masc. pluperf Kal. Comp. Heb. עָתַק.
iprutsu, "they broke," 3rd plu. masc. aor. Kal. Comp. Heb. פָּרַץ.
mamit-sun, "their oaths or fealty." Comp. Heb. אֲמָנָה, "a covenant."

35. DHAB-*ti*, subs. plu. fem. Comp. Heb. טוֹב.

36. *dababti*, "seditions." Comp. Heb. דבה "slander," "calmuny."
surrāti, "bold," "daring." Comp. Heb. שׁוּר "an enemy."
dababti, surrati idbubu = "with daring seditions they slandered."
idbubu, 3rd plu. masc. aor. Kal. Comp. Heb. דָּבַב.
milic, "counsel." Comp. Chald. מִלְכָּא.
imlicu, 3rd plu. masc. aor. Kal.

37. *ina citu*, "in agreement ;" *citu* = *cintu*, from כון.
va-attuni, "and, as for us;" *asabani minu*, "our seats (thrones) are numbered."
minu, 3rd plu. permansive. Heb. מָנָה.

39. *lissacin*, 3rd sing. masc. Prec Niphal. Heb. שכן.
akhai, "each other."

40. *nizūz*, "we will strengthen ;" lit. "we will fix."
ai-ibbasi, "may there not be ;" *ai* negative particle of deprecation "let it not." Comp. Heb. אִי. Job xxii. 30. *ibbasi niph.* from *basu*, "to exist," "to be."
kasrīnni, or *kasaranni*, "this bond, alliance, treaty, or conspiracy." Comp. Heb. קָשַׁר "to conspire ;" קֶשֶׁר "conspiracy."
sanūv, "another ;" lit. "a second." Comp. Heb. שֵׁנִי with mimmation.

41. *isteniahu*, "they devised." Comp. Heb. שׁנה, "to repeat."
LIMUT-*tiv*, "evil," "wicked ;" *amat limmutio*, "an evil conspiracy."

43. *D.P.* SUPAR-SAKI, "generals."

44. *siprāti*. Comp. Arab. *sapara*, "to send," subs. plur.

46. *ikhdhū*, 3rd plu. masc. aor. Kal. Comp. Heb. חָטָא.

47. *katus-sūn* for *katu-sun*, "their hands."

49. TUR = *tsākhru* (Heb. צָעִיר small). *W.A.I.*, ii. 48-20.

50. *yubluni*, 3rd plu. masc. pluper. Kal. Comp. Heb. יָבַל.

51. *munsakh damkati*, "bestower of favours" (Smith), but rather "taker away"(נסח).

52. KAR-BEL-MATATI, "the fortress of the lord of the world."

53. *riemu*, "mercy," "compassion." Comp. Heb. רֶחֶם.

LINE

arsi, "I showed." 1st sing. masc. aor. Kal.

citti for *cinti,* "covenant." Comp. Heb. כּוּן.

54. *eli-sa-makhri,* "more than before."

55. *lubulti* for *lubusti,* "clothing." Comp. Heb. לָבַשׁ.

birme, "variegated." Comp. Heb. בְּרוֹמִים (Ezek. xxvii. 24), "variegated garments." The Arabic cognate means "a cord twisted of two colours."

ulabbiśu for *ulabbis-su,* "I clothed him."

56. GUSKI = *Khuratsu,* "gold." Comp. Heb. חָרוּץ.

57. KHAR = *esiru,* "bracelet." Comp. Heb. שֵׁרָה, "chains," "bracelets."

uraccisa, 1st sing. masc. aor. Pael. Comp. Heb. רָכַם, "I fastened on."

58. RUM = *littu,* "sword." Sayce, *Syll.*, No. 11. Heb. לַהַט, Shaph.

sibbi. Mr. Norris (*Dict.* p. 725) compares Arab. *shaph,* "to polish," "to sharpen."

akhzu-su, "its handle," or, according to Mr. Smith, "sheath." Comp. Heb. אָחַז "to take hold of." The signs lost by the lacuna after *sum-ya* are, perhaps, *as-dhur-su,* "I wrote upon it." That it was the custom to engrave upon swords is proved by inspection of that lent by Colonel Hanbury for exhibition at the British Museum:—"The sword has had a richly jewelled hilt, which has been inlaid with ivory."—*Trans. Soc. Bib. Arch.*, iv. p. 348.

adin-su, "I gave him." 1st sing. masc. aor. Kal. for *addin.* Comp. Heb. נָתַן. The whole line reads, "(upon) a polished sword (having) a jewelled handle the account of my glory I wrote, and I gave (it) to him."

59. *D.P.*-RUCUBI, "chariots." Comp. Heb. רֶכֶב.

62. MASGAN-*isu,* "his district, or habitation." See *W.A.I.*, ii. 29, 18.

67. NIN = *bieltu.* *W.A.I.*, ii. 7, 19. Comp. Heb. בַּעֲלַת.

68. *yupakhir,* "he gathered." Heb. בחר.

ellat-śu, "his forces. Comp. Heb. חַיִל.

69. *yusatbā,* 3rd sing. masc. aor. Istaphal. Comp. Heb. בּוֹא, "to come."

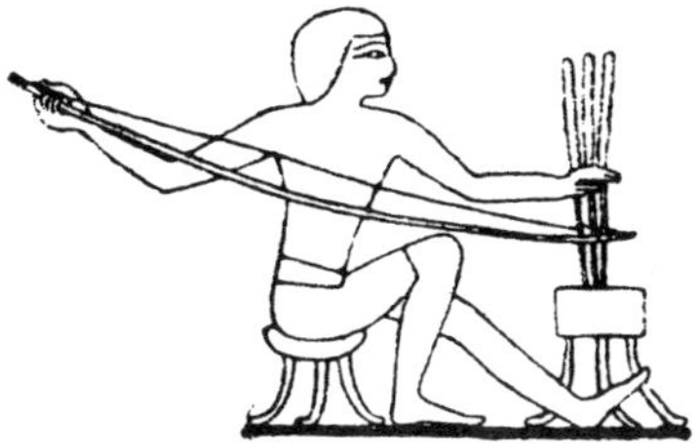

Reference Books

The Ancient World with special emphasis on Egyptology

ARES PUBLISHERS

612 N. MICHIGAN AVENUE
SUITE 216
CHICAGO, ILLINOIS 60611

DIRECTIONS FOR ORDERING
(see next page)

We will be very happy to process immediately your prepaid order (we accept your personal check* or money order), but PLEASE follow the directions listed below:

1) Bill procedures and bookkeeping costs have established a $10.00 *minimum* for prepaid mail orders. To this amoung please add $1.00 for postage and handling.

2) Libraries, schools, academic faculty and research scholars in U.S. *and overseas,* can order on open account ($20.00 minimum) providing that they write their order on their institutional letterhead.

3) For orders from $100.00 to $1,000.00 there is no postage or handling charge to the costumer paying list-prices for his books. Dealers and libraries pay postage.

4) Since we cannot be responsible for losses or damages in the Post-Office, we advise our costumers who order books of value above $100.00 to ask for *insurance* or *registration.* (Both at their own expense. Count $3.00 per package).

5) Books temporarily out of stock (*TOS*) or Not yet Published (*NYP*) are automatically back-ordered. If you desire an automatic refund for books of those categories in your prepaid order please note *PLEASE REFUND FOR TOS or NYP.* If you still wish to receive the book(s) when they are in stock or published and be billed, add the following: *BACKORDER IN O.A.*

6) Please: Do not forget to write on your order *the address* where you want us to mail the books. This way you will not be angry for not receiving your books and you will not occupy space in our *Absent-minded* file.

* NOTE FOR OVERSEAS CUSTOMERS. Our bank subtracts a minimum of $7.00 from every foreign currency check. So please pay by a check in U.S. $ (easy to obtain from your bank) or with an International Money Order.

CATALOGUE OF THE EGYPTIAN HIEROGLYPHIC PRINTING TYPE.
Alan H. Gardiner.

An amazing collection of tables which provide instant identification of all the Egyptian hieroglyphs. Arranged by type, such as "Gods," "Goddesses," "Birds," "Parts of Animals," a glance at the index shows exactly where to find the hieroglyphs which you wish to decipher. Useful introductory section and listing of Egyptian alphabet.

ISBN 0-89005-098-8 .... **$6.00**

EGYPTIAN READINGBOOK: Exercises and Middle Egyptian Texts. *Selected & Edited by Dr. A. De Buck.*

The Egyptian Readingbook, compiled by one of the best Egyptologists of the University of Leyden, is a unique collection of literary, religious, and private texts written in hieroglyphics. The student who has worked with Budge's, *Egyptian Language* or Mercer's *Grammar* needs the texts in the 'Readingbook' for study and practice.

ISBN 0-89005-213-1, 220pp. 8½ x 11 .... **$20.00**

PAPER AND BOOKS IN ANCIENT EGYPT. *J. Cerny.*

The revolution that the invention of the book brought to the cultures of the ancient people of the Near-East and the Mediterranean started in Egypt. It was under the shade of the Megalithic Egyptian temples, that the first 'papyrus scroll' was developed and in the great libraries of the Ptolemaic period that the idea of the 'papyrus codex' was born many centuries later. Without the Egyptian thought and thinkers, writing could still be limited to materials that could have delayed considerably the expansion of information, education and learning.

Prof. Cerny's account of 'Paper and Books in Ancient Egypt,' is the most complete, documented and dependable study available. In its compact form, it contains more information and facts than any other reference work on the subject.

ISBN 0-89005-205-0, 37pp. **$5.00**

TEN YEARS DIGGING IN EGYPT. *Flinders Petrie.*

A most fascinating account by the premier Egyptologist describing some of the most important discoveries in Egypt at the end of the 19th century. Illustrated with the drawings of the author.

ISBN 0-89005-107-0. 250pp. **$10.00**
Student edition **$6.00**

HISTORICAL SCARABS. *Flinders Petrie.*

The pocket handbook for the historian and collector of scarabs, with original drawings by Petrie. A useful primer to Newberry's *Ancient Egyptian Scarabs*. Includes 69 plates.

ISBN 0-89005-122-4. 84pp. **$10.00**
Student edition **$6.00**

ANCIENT EGYPTIAN SCARABS. *P. Newberry.*

A concise work covering all aspects of scarabs, cylinder seals, signet rings and other seals used by the ancient Egyptian. Indispensable reference work for scholars and collectors.

ISBN 0-89005-092-9 . . . . *$10.00*
Student edition *$6.00*

CULTS AND CREEDS IN GRAECO-ROMAN EGYPT. *H. Idris Bell.*

Valuable information from ancient papyri on the previously confused history of the religions and cults of Graeco-Roman Egypt. Special selections on the pagan amalgam, Jews in Egypt and the rise of Christianity.

ISBN 0-89005-088-0. x + 117pp. *$10.00*
Student edition *$6.00*

INSCRIPTIONES GRAECAE AEGYPTI: INSCRIPTIONES NUNC CAIRO IN MUSEO. *C. Milne.*

The Greek inscriptions of Egypt included in this volume, originally published in the *Catalogue General des Antiquities Egyptiennes du Musee du Caire,* are here for the first time technically incorporated in the *Inscriptiones Graecae* along with the author's excellent commentaries.

ISBN 0-89005-111-9. 169pp. *$25.00*

INSCRIPTIONES GRAECAE PTOLEMAICAE I. *Max L. Strack.*

The first collection of Ptolemaic inscriptions not limited to the political boundaries of the Empire, but including inscriptions from all areas which came under the radiating influence of its culture. Also appearing is an appendix which includes tables for the "Names and Epithets of the Kings," his "Chronological List of the Kings," plus several commentaries.

ISBN 0-89005-171-2. 120pp. *$10.00*

The new series of the BIBLIOTHECA AEGYPTIACA is only a part of our publishing program of reprinting and publishing new books on the ANCIENT WORLD. Our 1977 catalogue lists more than 150 books in this special area, with emphasis on the ANCIENT NEAR EAST, the ANCIENT MEDITERRANEAN, ANCIENT GREECE, the HELLENISTIC WORLD and the WORLD OF ROME. If you are interested, send us a postcard with your name and address. We will mail to you a FREE copy.

ARES PUBLISHERS Inc.

612 NORTH MICHIGAN AVE., SUITE 216
CHICAGO, ILLINOIS 60611

FROM 1974 TO 1978, WE HAVE NOT RAISED OUR PRICES DESPITE THE FACT THAT OUR EXPENSES ARE CONSIDERABLY HIGHER THAN THEY WERE IN 1974. *YOU KNOW* THAT ALL OTHER PUBLISHERS DID NOT FOLLOW THIS POLICY AND MANY OF THEM *ASK PRICES THAT YOU CANNOT AFFORD.*

YOU CAN HELP TO KEEP PRICES DOWN

I. ORDER THE BOOKS YOU WANT FROM OUR LIST *DIRECTLY FROM US.*

II. ASK YOUR PUBLIC LIBRARY TO ORDER BOOKS FROM ARES. TELL THEM TO *ORDER DIRECT* FOR BETTER SERVICE. *LIBRARIES ARE BILLED FOR ANY AMOUNT.*

III. ASK YOUR UNIVERSITY OR COLLEGE LIBRARY TO ORDER THE BOOKS THAT YOU CONSIDER NECESSARY FOR THE REFERENCE AND SPECIAL COLLECTIONS. FILL THE SLIPS AND MARK THEM *ORDER DIRECTLY FROM PUBLISHER.*

IV. SEND US THE ADDRESSES OF YOUR FRIENDS AND COLLEAGUES SO THAT WE WILL MAIL CATALOGUES TO THEM.

V. IF YOU ARE A TEACHER OR UNIVERSITY PROFESSOR, DO CONSIDER OUR BOOKS FOR THE COURSES YOU TEACH.

VI. ASK YOUR UNIVERSITY OR COLLEGE BOOK SHOP TO ORDER SOME OF OUR BOOKS AS PART OF THEIR GENERAL STOCK. THIS REQUEST WILL HELP A LOT OF STUDENTS AND FACULTY TO LEARN ABOUT OUR PUBLISHING PROGRAM.

VII. WRITE TO US! SUGGEST TITLES FOR REPRINTING, NEW WORKS FOR PUBLISHING. WE NEED YOUR IDEAS.

VIII. IF YOU NEED TO BUY BOOKS ($75.00 and above) AND PAY FOR THEM IN MONTHLY PAYMENTS, DO WRITE TO US. WE ARE *PEOPLE,* NOT COMPUTERS.

ARES PUBLISHERS Inc.

612 NORTH MICHIGAN AVE., SUITE 216
CHICAGO, ILLINOIS 60611

ORDER FORM

Name ____

Address ______________________________________

City____________________ State ________ Zip ________

Author	Title	Quantity	Price

Postage and Handling	
State Tax (Residents only)	
Total	

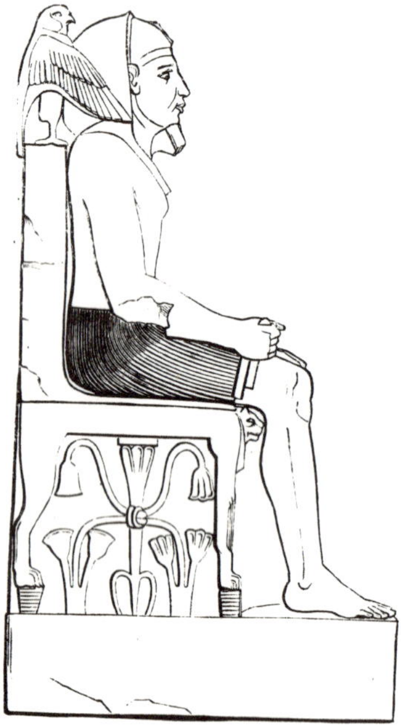

Portrait-statue of King Chephren.
(Ancient Kingdom.)